Praise for

WE ARE ALL
paralyzed

"A wonderful example of unwavering faith in God's plan for us, Brandon Sulser gives reassurance that our Lord will help us carry our burdens and not forsake us."

—MARK "OZ" GEIST, bestselling coauthor of *13 Hours* and security and military consultant. Geist is credited with saving twenty-five people in the attack on Benghazi.

"I am convinced Brandon is an angel among us to remind us what pure faith looks like. His story is heartbreaking but also heroic. He is a textbook example of a true disciple of God who shows his love for God and his fellow men through service, faith, and perseverance."

—TIM BALLARD, founder of Operation Underground Railroad

"While Brandon is singularly unique and the challenges he endured are one in a million, the life lessons he imparts are universal. Anyone can relate to the struggle to overcome difficulties with grace, let alone with joy! And it is that joy, empathy, and light that come through in Brandon's book. It was a great read that I would highly recommend."

—SANDRA N. TILLOTSON, founder and senior vice president of Nu Skin

"My friend Brandon's story is inspiring, to say the least. I have learned much from rubbing shoulders with him these past few years and his trademark indomitable spirit shines through every word on every page. I was pleased to find that he is as captivating a writer as he is a speaker. We would all do well to learn from Brandon."

—JOHN LAUCK, president and CEO of Children's Miracle Network

"An amazing and inspiring comeback story that is a must read for anyone seeking peace and understanding through heartache. Brandon offers a valuable perspective of joy and hope in an often-uncomfortable life journey. The lessons he learned from facing challenges and never giving up have the power to change lives."

—COLLIN RAYE, twenty-four top-ten records, sixteen number-one hits, ten-time CMA and ACM nominee

WE ARE ALL
paralyzed

The Remarkable True Story
of Choosing to Live after
FOUR LIFE-THREATENING ACCIDENTS

BRANDON SULSER
with KATE LEE

PLAIN SIGHT
PUBLISHING
An imprint of Cedar Fort, Inc.
Springville, Utah

ISBN 13: 978-1-4621-2350-6

Published by Plain Sight Publishing, an imprint of Cedar Fort, Inc.
2373 W. 700 S., Springville, UT 84663
Distributed by Cedar Fort, Inc., www.cedarfort.com

LIBRARY OF CONGRESS CATALOGING-IN-PUBLICATION DATA

Names: Sulser, Brandon, 1979- author.
Title: We are all paralyzed / Brandon Sulser.
Description: Springville, Utah : Plain Sight Publishing, An imprint of Cedar
    Fort, Inc., [2019]
Identifiers: LCCN 2019004435 (print) | LCCN 2019012866 (ebook) | ISBN
    9781462131068 (epub, pdf, mobi) | ISBN 9781462123506 (perfect bound : alk.
    paper)
Subjects: LCSH: Sulser, Brandon, 1979- | Mormons--Biography. |
    Paralytics--Rehabilitation--Personal narratives. | Resilience (Personality
    trait) | Suffering--Religious aspects--Church of Jesus Christ of
    Latter-day Saints.
Classification: LCC BX8695.S89 (ebook) | LCC BX8695.S89 A3 2019 (print) |
    DDC 289.3092 [B] --dc23
LC record available at https://lccn.loc.gov/2019004435

Cover design by Jeff Harvey
Cover design © 2019 Cedar Fort, Inc.
Edited by Valene Wood and Nicole Terry
Typeset by Kaitlin Barwick

Printed in the United States of America

10 9 8 7 6 5 4 3 2 1

Printed on acid-free paper

Contents

"The Lord gave, and the Lord hath taken away;
blessed be the name of the Lord."

Job 1:21

Chapter 1

THE BEGINNING

My lips were sore and my mouth was bone dry as I rapidly rode my mountain bike down Mueller Park Canyon. My Boy Scout troop and I were all exhausted from an overnight camping trip to Rudy's Flat, a campsite nestled high above the canyon. I paused for a moment to drink the last remaining drops of water from my canteen. Just finishing our two-day trip, we'd reached the end of the trail. Open road was all that separated us from our homes a mile away.

"Go ahead, guys," I told the other Scouts. "I'll catch up in a minute."

Catching up had been heavily on my mind the past few months and was something I had desperately desired to do since moving from Littleton, Colorado, to Bountiful, Utah, with my family.

In Colorado I had it good. The year was 1993, and I had just won the school talent show—assisted in great part by my MC Hammer pants. I did my best "running man" while the bouncing of my oversized gold chain hypnotized the audience.

As "U Can't Touch This" came to its glorious end, the chanting of the prepubescent girls only proved to me, my brother, and our two friends what we already knew: we had won by a landslide. If that weren't enough, I had just heard that Nikki, the cutest girl at school, liked me, confirmed by a note one of her friends had shown my friends. I was living the good life for a sixth grader in the Mile High City.

Living in Colorado taught me some valuable lessons, like not letting cultural or religious differences serve as justification to forgo lasting friendships. Some of my best friends had different religious beliefs and upbringings from me. One was Jewish, another was Buddhist, and I was Christian, and we all got along beautifully.

My friends knew that I didn't swear, and they respected me for it. I would often marvel at how quickly the environment would change when we were all together. Instead of cuss words, there were a lot of goshes and darns. Every once in a while, a swear word would slip in, but immediately my friends would apologize.

Though none of them were actively religious, they were great kids. To them, going to a Denver Broncos football game each Sunday was the same as going to church was to me. It was a weekly occurrence that none of us missed.

With those memories fresh in my mind, my thoughts turned to my first few weeks of school in Utah and the vast difference between the two states. As a twelve-year-old, I felt like I had fallen from the top of the food chain in popularity and stature in Colorado to the bottom in Utah. With living in a new house, attending a new school, and trying to find new friends, I was struggling immensely to fit in, a problem that was completely foreign to me.

It seemed that whatever efforts I made to develop friendships were not reciprocated that first year. I couldn't understand why. Here I was living in a place where roughly 90 percent of the kids were culturally and religiously just like me, yet I was struggling. I reasoned that because I grew up out of state, I didn't fit the mold or the cliques that had already been established. To me, these kids knew nothing of change, nor did they know how to accept it. Eventually, I understood that wasn't the case. Being born and raised inside the same homes in the same neighborhoods, many of them just hadn't had the opportunity to understand what it felt like to be the new kid. They weren't necessarily trying to exclude me; they just weren't trying to include me. Consequently, people didn't really know who I was.

One day at school, after walking to the bathroom, I noticed a list somebody had taped on the bathroom mirror. It read, "The Hottest Boys in the 6th Grade." The list, written by a few of the sixth-grade girls, was numbered one through fifteen. My eyes perked up with excitement as I began scanning the list in hopes that my name was on it. As my finger slid down the list, my confidence and self-esteem sunk along with it. My name was not on the sheet. I yearned for verification that I not only existed at this school but also was *liked*. I looked at myself in the mirror and then back at the list, and my head fell low. Reluctantly I walked back to my new classroom, wishing I were back in Colorado.

Thinking about those experiences as I rested on my mountain bike brought back feelings of being less than who I really was and wanted to be. This was the first time in my young life that

I'd been subjected to the feelings of being socially isolated. I hated the way it felt, and I vowed to never exclude others.

Placing my feet back on the pedals of my mountain bike, I determined to catch up to the Boy Scouts ahead—not just on this trail but also socially. As I took off down the mountain once again, I planned to develop new and lasting friendships during my summer break.

Mueller Park Canyon in the early summer morning is a sight to behold. The fresh mountain air combined with the scents of the pine, aspen, and maple trees could be the best natural potpourri there is. Highlighted by a babbling brook that snaked along the bike trail, the mountains were alive with a chorus of songbirds welcoming the new day.

All of a sudden, I noticed a change. Something was definitely different. To this day, I do not know how to describe what happened to me. It was almost as if my senses became extremely heightened. The beauty, the smells, and the feeling around me instantly became overpowering, so much so that I stopped my bike and offered a prayer of gratitude. I felt a profound sense of peace from my Savior and His creations unlike anything my twelve-year-old self had ever felt before. It was as if I could sense something big was going to happen in my life. Alone and in awe, I hesitantly returned to my bike, not wanting to leave this sacred spot and fearing that when I did, this heavenly feeling would end. But knowing I needed to catch up to the others, I began to bike down the hill toward home.

That's when everything went black.

"Son, don't move. We have you in a neck brace and are taking you to the hospital."

Confused, I opened my eyes. My moment of spiritual bliss had quickly evaporated into an overwhelming sense of physical pain ripping through my head. I could feel that my shirt was soaking wet. From the aching in my head, I knew it was blood.

"What happened?" I asked, feeling panic begin to rush through me as I saw a paramedic kneeling above me.

"You've had a really bad bicycle accident," the man responded. "Are you in any pain or discomfort?"

"I just have a really bad headache," I told him. "I'm seeing double, and I feel like I'm going to throw up."

Another paramedic spoke up. "You've been unconscious for ten minutes," he said. "You're likely having symptoms of a severe concussion. The blood is coming from a pretty bad hematoma. We are going to need to take you to the hospital."

I knew I was hurt badly, but it was odd—the only thing I wanted to do was tell them about the amazing spiritual experience I had just had. As the paramedics put me on the gurney, I noticed for the first time that I was surrounded by my Boy Scout troop and leaders, all anxiously wondering what had happened. There was a lady there too. She was explaining that she was the one who'd found me. I heard her say that she had been showering in her home when she heard the crash. Looking out her bathroom window, she saw me lying limp on the sidewalk.

Apparently I had blacked out somehow while riding my bike. Thrown over my handlebars, I hit the corner of the concrete curb surrounding the sidewalk headfirst.

Despite all I was feeling, I kept trying to tell anyone that would listen about my spiritual experience, but they were too caught up in attending to me. Finally, before the paramedics were going to load me into the ambulance, I said, "Wait! I have to tell you something before I go."

However, both the paramedics and my Boy Scout leader told me that I'd have plenty of time to talk once they got me to the hospital. Frustrated but in too much pain to argue, I stopped trying.

"I'll call your parents and let them know what's happened," my leader assured me. "They'll meet you there."

I gave a half-hearted wave goodbye as the ambulance doors shut. Not five minutes later, I arrived at the hospital.

The concern on my parents' faces was evident as they rushed up to grab my hand after I was unloaded from the ambulance.

"Mom, I need to tell you something that I saw!" I said excitedly. Much to my frustration, however, I was whisked away before I could tell her. Several hours went by of medical testing and X-rays before I saw my parents again. After they had been assured that I was okay, my mom asked me what it was that I had wanted to tell her. Thinking for a moment, I could only recall the feelings of heightened spiritual senses leading up to some incredible heavenly experience that I could no longer remember. Instantly I started to tear up. "I forgot, Mom!" I said, desperately wanting to recall the images of something I could still feel radiating inside of me. "Oh no! I forgot!"

Urgently, I riffled through my memory for any clues to awaken the experience. Like trying to pry open a heavy door with no handle, my mind would not release what it held there. I often look back and wonder if this was, in fact, reality in the physical sense or if something else happened to me, like a vision, or even if I was taken somewhere. Years later and now knowing what my life would become, I can't help but wonder if whatever happened to me wasn't meant to be remembered but the sacred feelings surrounding it were. Perhaps my spirit needed to be reminded that God loved me and that my life had meaning long before I would question all of it. Maybe the beginning of our heartache is also the beginning of His.

Since then, I've been up that canyon multiple times. To this day, I still can't find the spot where I felt that peace and serenity.

However, what happened later that night would change my life forever.

Chapter 2

KEEP ME HERE

I was suffering from a terrible, pounding headache, and walking only made it worse. As we left the hospital and drove home, the crushing, throbbing, and extreme dizziness overwhelmed me. I could barely stand straight as I got out of the car. With my parents supporting me on either side, it took a while to get me in the house and downstairs. Feeling unbelievably weak, I told my parents that I needed to lie down. It felt as if my head had suddenly become tremendously heavy and I could no longer support its weight.

Once my parents helped me lie down on the couch, I could see that they were very concerned. However, they trusted the doctor's assessment that I had a severe concussion and that things would get better with time. But it wasn't just the pain that had me feeling miserable.

My mom had told me at least ten different times to pack my helmet before I left on the campout. Remembering how foolish I'd been in choosing to ignore her only made my head hurt more. Overwhelmed with emotion, I told my parents, "I'm so sorry I was so stupid. I should've listened to you. I'll never do that again." The only excuse I had for not taking my helmet was peer pressure—I knew the other boys and the Scout leaders wouldn't be wearing theirs. Feeling that this trip was my chance to regain what I had lost in Colorado, I threw common sense out the window, trading it instead for the false sense of security that comes with fitting in.

As I lay on the couch feeling awful, the hours slowly passed and things got considerably worse. I had begun throwing up and could not stop. I was also having difficulty seeing straight. It literally felt like something in my brain was going to rupture. I wasn't a pretty sight either. The right side of my head started to swell noticeably. Running my fingers against the side of my scalp, I felt them sink in as if pressing down on a waterbed. Hoping cold would reduce the swelling, I put an ice pack on my head, but it gave no relief.

At roughly 10:30 that evening, I knew I was not okay. Even at my young age, I felt odd and suddenly aware that angels and heaven were within my grasp. Death was close. I had already developed a strong belief in the teachings of Jesus Christ. Because I was born to wonderful parents who taught me His gospel, I never doubted any of it: the scriptures, my Savior Jesus Christ's Atonement, and the teaching that even after death families can be together forever. Having that faith gave me insight into and hope about where I would go, should I die that night. Yet even though I had that sacred knowledge, my fears of dying began to escalate as the night moved on, and the pain grew unbearable.

By this time, my mom and dad were both by my side, holding my hands. With tears in my eyes, I began to plead with them. "I feel like I have to hold in my spirit from leaving my body," I said. "I'm scared. I don't want to die right now!" As I spoke the words, the color in my face suddenly began to fade dramatically, only confirming what I was saying. It was as if my spirit were a helium-filled balloon. I had to mentally and physically fight to keep it from escaping my body. I felt that at any time if I were to "let go," I would cross over to heaven.

Feeling death was imminent, I asked my dad to give me a blessing that God might preserve my life. After my father had given me the blessing, I felt a sudden relief that my spirit was no longer yearning to leave my body. With the fear of dying no longer present, I closed my eyes and tried to get some sleep, but nothing could relieve my pain. My parents stayed by my side the entire night, providing strength and comfort. Early the next morning, when I still hadn't improved, it became evident that we needed to rush back to the hospital.

Once we arrived, a doctor took one look at me and determined that I would need a CT scan. Lying still in the small tube that conjures up feelings of claustrophobia even for those who are not claustrophobic, I suddenly heard a frantic voice yelling to the radiologist to call for Life Flight. Moments later, I was being rushed out the door.

"Brandon may literally have minutes to live if he's not operated on immediately!" I heard my doctor say as he passed my startled parents on the way to the helipad.

"What do you mean?!" was my mom's frantic reply as she and my dad tried to keep pace with the gurney. "You told us it was just a bad concussion!" I could hear the fear and anger rising in her voice.

"The X-ray missed a large subdural hematoma last night," the doctor explained. "We should've done a CT scan."

"That was over twenty-four hours ago!" my mom cried.

As we got to the helipad and waited for the helicopter to arrive, my parents fired off a barrage of questions. They wanted guarantees that I would be okay and that the doctors were sure of what they were seeing this time. The ER doctor responded quickly. "Look, there are no guarantees," he said, "but if you want your son to have a chance at living, he needs to be operated on immediately." He quickly continued, "The blood pressure inside his head is literally pushing his brain down his spine. He needs to go to Primary Children's Hospital now for life-saving surgery."

I could clearly see the "freak-out-o-meter" go off on my parents' faces. To be honest, mine was off the charts. But while I definitely had thoughts of this being the last time I would see my parents again, I had faith in the blessing I had received the night before. Not only that, but I still remembered the sacred experience I had had before my accident. I knew I was in the Lord's hands. Whatever the outcome, it was His outcome, and that brought me peace. I chose to have faith, and so did my parents.

Quickly, we spoke of the miracle we had witnessed after my blessing. For us it was evidence enough that the Lord didn't preserve my life that night only for me to lose it while on Life Flight. With tears in my eyes, I waved goodbye to my parents, not knowing what my life would be like when I saw them again.

Opening my eyes, I found myself in a hospital room post-surgery. Again, my parents were on either side of the bed, holding my hands.

"The surgeons said the surgery went great," my dad said. "They said you're a miracle."

Looking around, I quickly became alarmed by all the medical devices and the beeping sounds surrounding my bed. Sensing my sudden anxiety, my dad tried to calm me down. "It's okay. We'll get through this together, Brandon," he said.

"The important thing is that you made it. With time, everything will work out."

Wondering what had been done to me, I asked my parents to bring me a mirror.

As I held it up to my face, I was shocked at what looked back at me. In their rush, the nurses had haphazardly shaved my head. Small tufts of hair that had been missed poked between drainage tubes inserted into both sides of my head, while staples formed a frightening path from one ear to another. With tears streaming down my face, I stared, horrified at my reflection.

"They've turned me into Frankenstein," I said.

I would spend four weeks in the hospital that time, recovering from the nearly eight-hour-long brain surgery. Although I can't recall what took place during most of those four weeks, I do vividly remember the neurosurgeon coming into the hospital room to speak to my family and me after the operation.

He began to explain to us that to get to my brain, he'd surgically removed a piece of bone from my skull, hoping to relieve the built-up pressure from the blood. After this was done, he and the other surgeons fully expected to see that my main artery had ruptured and was still pushing blood into my head. Once they had found my torn artery, however, they were shocked to discover that it was completely plugged, sealed off by a blood clot and no longer bleeding. This was highly unusual and nothing they had ever seen before. The surgeon then explained that the clot looked as though it had likely formed the night before. Looking at me pointedly, he spoke again. "I planned on saving your life today, but someone else beat me to it," he said. "If the artery had simply bled at its normal rate, you would have died last night. He then told me, "Someone from the other side must have stepped in to save you. All we did was relieve the blood pressure and place some titanium screws to hold your cracked head together."

As I contemplated what had happened, the neurosurgeon turned to my parents and explained that people usually die hours after an accident as severe as mine and that everyone who had been in the operating room was amazed that it had been over twenty-four hours and I was still alive. Turning to me again, he said, "I'm not necessarily religious, but if miracles do happen, this was definitely one of them."

Without saying anything, my parents and I understood that this truly was a miracle.

Although my life had been spared, the doctors warned me that I was now at the beginning of what could be a very long uphill battle. My brain had sustained a major TBI, or traumatic brain injury. As a result, my learning, speaking, and thinking were all impaired.

Little did I know that my desire to catch up with my new friends and peers in Utah that day would affect my entire life. This would become evident once I got home. My life had truly changed. Mentally I was not the same. Emotionally I was not the same either. Asking God to save my life that night would not be the last time I would pray for a miracle. In fact, it would be the first of many.

Chapter 3

TBI AND JUNIOR HIGH

Living with a TBI is like having an annoying houseguest who's come over uninvited and won't leave. It causes you to be emotionally erratic, mentally drained, lethargic, and depressed.

I was petrified. I knew eventually summer would end. Then one of my biggest challenges would begin: junior high. Middle school is already hard enough; middle school with a brain injury is almost impossible. I was still in bad shape. Not only did I look horrible, but I also couldn't respond quickly enough to escape under the junior-high radar, making me the perfect target.

Most of my problems stemmed from my brain's inability to visually and mentally process information quickly. Math and English suddenly became extremely difficult for me to not only figure out but also retain. Just walking around my house processing all the various sights and sounds made my head feel like I had just run a marathon. I wondered how in the world I could do something as complicated as math. To add insult to injury, the accident also caused me to speak with a noticeable stutter. All of that along with the almost constant companionship of severe migraines and double vision caused me so much social anxiety that there were times I thought about ending it all.

Looking at my reflection in the mirror one day and staring back at somebody I hardly recognized was haunting. I looked like a prisoner of war. I had lost significant weight. My head was shaved, and I had a large scar. It was a battlefield on my head, with a noticeable DMZ line landscaped across my naked scalp.

My plan that summer of regaining my mojo from Colorado and re-establishing friends in Utah was hijacked. The worst part was knowing that it all could've been avoided, had I just made the right decision to wear my helmet, something I beat myself up about regularly.

Just prior to school starting, my doctor recommended that I be evaluated to see if my cognition was adequate to begin seventh grade. This process took nearly a week and was designed to test memory retention, intellectual fatigue, and processing skills. Each day, I endured roughly four hours of testing, by the end of which I was mentally fatigued. Though my mind was exhausted, my body was full of youthful energy. While my mind screamed for me to sleep, my body yelled, "Let's move!"— leaving me feeling continually restless.

My test results were humbling; many of them showed I was at a third-grade level. Fear struck. "I just graduated from elementary school," I stuttered. "I'm n-na-not going back!" I defiantly finished. The person running the tests looked at me sympathetically before informing us that the state of Utah had a school transition and re-entry program for kids with TBIs. If I wanted to go to junior high, it would be necessary for me to attend resource or classes designed for kids with special learning needs. I was not thrilled with the idea, but with no other choice, it was decided that I would have a resource period daily to help with homework and tutoring. As a signing bonus, the neuropsychologist mentioned that my memory and processing skills were so impaired that I would be exempt from the high school requirement of taking two years of a foreign language. Plus, I would be given extra time to finish homework and take tests. After hearing that, I smiled mischievously. I had just been given a "get out of jail free" card. Quickly turning my smile into a frown, I looked at my neuropsychologist. Stuttering and trying to look forlorn, I said, "Tell me again, how much extra time do I ha-ha-have to finish my homework?"

My first day of seventh grade was an absolute disaster. It wasn't like I was returning to friends who already knew, accepted, and liked me. I wasn't just the new kid—I was the new kid who wore a baseball cap and had no team to back me up. I was constantly worried about my new shortcomings, and all I wanted in those first few weeks was to blend into the crowd unnoticed. Unfortunately, I stuck out like a sore thumb, plus I had the worry of every other seventh-grade boy: what if I got shoved in a locker? Even though that was a rumor, for me the idea of someone, even jokingly, pushing me and causing me to hit my head was a legitimate life-and-death possibility. My parents had me under strict surveillance because my head was still healing. Any sudden jolt or movement could cause the artery in my brain to rupture again, undoing everything surgery had just fixed. Now my fate was literally in the hands of a bunch of kids with little to no decision-making skills.

On the first day of school, my mom dropped me off. I'm sure she was just as nervous for me as I was that day. Reluctantly exiting the car, I slowly made my way toward Millcreek Junior High School's front doors. Briefly glancing at my mom, I wished she'd yell at me to come back and tell me that I wasn't ready, that I could go home, where I was safe. There wasn't anything I would've rather done. Instead, I got a confident smile and a thumbs up before she drove away.

What I would not understand until I was an adult was what lay behind that smile. That smile masked both of my parents' greatest uncertainties and worries. Millions of fears swirled ominously in my mom's head as she watched me walk away from her that morning. Would I make friends? Would I hit my head? Would the teachers remember to give me extra time? If there weren't friends to walk beside me, would there be angels watching over me?

While she drove away terrified, my dad was sitting at his office worrying. His greatest fear was that of a pack mentality and me being easy prey. My parents were sending Humpty Dumpty off to school each day, knowing there was a strong possibility that I would return physically and mentally broken. With my San Francisco Giants baseball cap on, I took a deep breath and opened the school doors, walking straight into the lion's den.

I hadn't even made it to my locker before a big ninth grader walked up to me. He ripped off my baseball cap and tossed it down the hall while yelling, "Hey, little seventh grader, hats aren't allowed at school!"

Time froze. The excited chatter of reacquainted friends came to a standstill as everyone at school stopped to watch the spectacle. Everything I had feared would happen was now my reality.

Immediately, another ninth grader pointed to my head. "Wow, dude!" he yelled loud enough for everyone to hear. "You look like Frankenstein!"

By this time, the hallway was crowded with kids looking at my exposed head. Full of embarrassment and anger, I wanted to run home. My scar and staples were still clearly visible—my hair was just starting to grow back. If I couldn't run home, then I at least wanted to fight back and show these bullies that I wasn't going to let them treat me this way. The doctor's warnings rung in my ears that any new head trauma could be my last. Forbidden to engage in anything that could cause it, I was physically powerless.

Because I could not react in anger, something amazing happened: I had to learn to be patient. As I slowly walked over to grab my hat, my mind quickly thought of something I could say. Shaking off what had just transpired as best I could, I forced a placid smile, like the one given to me earlier by my mom. Stuttering, I responded, "I had a severe ac-ac-accident and will be wa-wearing my hat until my hair grows back."

Word about my scar got around quickly after that. Soon everybody knew that the only boy who could wear a hat to junior high had something hiding underneath. I could hear the immediate whisperings as a firestorm of gossip burned out of control through the halls. I heard rumblings that parts of my brain were removed and that I was dying from brain cancer. I knew I had to get ahead of these tall tales and control my story the best I could. So I tried something unthinkable for a twelve-year-old: I chose to be open, honest, and confident about my looks and injury.

That same day, I flipped the script from being someone who had a weakness to being someone who was trying to be strong. I'd take off my ball cap whenever I was asked about my scar and act like it was a proud medal of honor. "That's not all," I'd say. "I also have two titanium screws over here." Pointing at my head, I'd instruct them, "Put your fa-fa-finger right here and feel for yourself."

My peers quickly realized that I wasn't dying and, more important, that I wasn't something to be afraid of. I was simply recovering, and my "cool scar" was proof of my miraculous story.

After those first six months, my staples were removed. My hair quickly grew back, covering up my scar, and I had made some great friends. On one hand, I was grateful to blend in with everyone else, but on the other hand, I didn't have visual validation of why I was stuttering or socially quiet. I looked and acted like everyone else now, but inside I was still struggling immensely.

When I tried communicating with others while in crowded and noisy hallways or even in small groups, the stimulus around me was overwhelming to my injured brain. Like a sponge already saturated with water, it was unable to absorb additional information quickly enough to keep up. In conversation, I instantly knew what I wanted to say, but by the time my words got out of my mouth the discussion had already moved on to something else. To compensate, I would try to force the words out quicker. Stuttering and awkward pauses were always the result.

My anxiety, mingled with my speaking difficulties, made talking to cute girls a recipe for disaster. I had no chance to respond or make sense out of anything. Watching and listening to junior high girls talk to each other is like standing in the middle of an active beehive. It's hard enough for anyone to keep up; for me it was impossible. I'd quickly short-circuit, leaving me wide-eyed and exhausted . . . Well, at least more than every other boy.

As the girls would wait for me to respond, I'd finally manage to say, "I'm sorry, wa-wa-what were you talking about?" In reply, they'd awkwardly move on to the next guy who could at least keep up with the conversation.

My junior high crush was a beautiful girl named Molly. She was big-hearted and kind, with blond hair and blue eyes—to me she was the whole package. I wasn't the only boy in school that was infatuated with her either. When her friend told my friend and my friend told me that she liked me too, I was elated.

At the end-of-the-year dance, I finally worked up the nerve to talk to Molly—not only that, but I decided to ask her to dance. This was no easy task in and of itself. The life of pretty girls at school dances isn't easy. Sure, they may have plenty of space and air during a fast song, but once the DJ drops a slow beat, they must brace themselves for the sudden influx of seventh-, eighth-, and ninth-grade boys. It was like we were schools of fish separated by grade and size; the seventh graders usually got the scraps, while the ninth graders always seemed to have first pick when a slow song began. These were the laws of the jungle that aren't written but are ingrained within the DNA code of boys.

I knew that I had to be fast and I had to be close to Molly to get any chance at a dance. Patiently, I waited for Howard Jones to sing the quintessential junior-high-dance song "No One Is to Blame." I yearned for Howard Jones to give me the break I had waited all year for as he sung the words my mouth could not form. Gracelessly, I danced close enough to Molly to get first dibs on the next slow song, but just far enough away not to be creepy. As the group Naughty by Nature concluded their last "hip hop hurray" and all hands fell back down to our sides, Molly looked at me and smiled. Taking a deep breath, I opened my mouth.

Nothing came out. It was as if my voice box ran away from me in terror. Molly moved closer to me. My mouth hung open and a look of sheer panic fell on my face. After some time, I finally managed to say, "I-I wa-was wondering . . ." Long pause. Suddenly an eighth-grade boy with a bowl cut that screamed "stay away from me" saw my distress and took full advantage. Swooping in, he confidently and flawlessly asked Molly to dance.

Before I could finish with, "Would you like to dance with me?" she was gone, in the arms of another boy. Embarrassed and devastated, I held in my tears as I quickly walked out of the gymnasium and into the boys' restroom. Sitting down in the safety of one of the stalls, I let the tears fall down my cheeks.

Grabbing my head in frustration, I cried out, "Work with me. I need you to be present, or I'm not going to make it." I needed something, anything, to show me that I was still capable of being the person I truly was within my soul. No longer just about Molly, everything came crashing down in that moment. Falling to my knees, I humbly asked my Father in Heaven for a victory over my challenges. Once I had finished, I knew what I had to do.

With my faith and confidence reinvigorated, I walked con-fidently back into that school gymnasium and asked Molly to dance. It went perfectly—no awkward pauses or stuttering. As I danced with her, I couldn't help but smile and thank the Lord for helping me that day.

This wasn't the only socially painful incident caused by my head injury. There were countless others during my junior high years and even into high school. The more they occurred, the more I withdrew myself socially. In self-preservation mode, living and feeling everything a guy my age went through but being unable to show who I truly was killed me inside and caused severe depression.

Through many prayers during those years I felt reassurance from my Heavenly Father that He knew my trial and loved me and that I should remain patient with my struggles until they no longer were an issue. I knew who I was; it was the fact that most of my peers didn't that hurt the most. When people see someone struggling to communicate or interact, they may naturally assume that person is unintelligent or socially awkward. I learned through my adversity to never judge a book by its cover, because there is a good chance the contents are worth the read.

It was humbling going to resource class every day and seeing others for who they were on a personal level without focusing on their disabilities. As bad as I thought my challenges were or as difficult as they seemed, I still had hope. In contrast, I saw kids from broken homes, with drug addictions, who were abused, and who had genuinely hard lives. Though they did not suffer from similar injuries to mine, their outlooks were dark, affecting how they learned and, consequently, how they chose to live. Surrounded by those kids, I quickly realized that I was blessed, despite my challenges. I had great, supportive parents who would console me on an almost daily basis as I opened up about my frustrations and challenges. Their love, wisdom, and guidance often saved me from going down paths of darkness I saw some of my peers take.

Choosing not to let my disability define me and, more important, choosing not to let others define me, I eventually learned to be confident in who I was. I would later come to realize why this lesson was so important for me to learn. Almost cyclical in nature, it seemed that I was destined to find myself only to lose myself again.

Chapter 4

STORM CHASER

There is a TV show that I used to love to watch called *Storm Chasers*, about individuals who were fascinated by dangerous weather. Instead of finding shelter and avoiding extreme storms, they would track, seek, and then chase after them. Thriving off the adrenaline rush that running toward this danger brings, they found that chasing these storms became addicting—so much so that after a while, simply chasing the storm was not enough. These chasers needed to get closer. When they finally realized the danger they were in, it was too late; the storm had over-taken them.

Though I wasn't a bad kid in my youth, I maybe could have been called a storm chaser. I loved to push boundaries and see what I could get away with, not because I liked causing trouble but because I liked challenges and risk. Where reasoning would normally talk most kids out of risky behavior, my TBI made me impulsive, and I rarely, if ever, considered consequences. Add to that the fact that I yearned to be noticed, and I often pushed boundaries.

One day, I met another storm chaser.

Recently moved from Idaho, Cameron Wright was a fearless, loud, big-hearted, funny, straight-shooting kid. With a dad who was the perfect embodiment of a cowboy, Cameron had been taught responsibility and how to work hard from a young age. Years before Cameron was sixteen and had his driver's license, it wasn't uncommon for Cameron's dad to send him down the hill in the pickup truck to go get gas for the snowmobiles or run an errand. I got the pleasure of riding along. We were boys that felt like men, which only added to our storm-chasing ways.

I remember getting a call once to come down to Cameron's house. At the end of the call, he quickly added, "Do you know how to gut and skin a deer?"

We weren't even teens yet. When I arrived, Cameron's dad was beaming with pride at the deer Cameron had shot in his own backyard, now hanging up in a tree. With no idea how to gut it, skin it, or divide the meat, Cameron and I did our best, divvying up the kill to the neighborhood kids in little Ziploc bags (we were both sick for weeks). When we weren't hunting, Cameron's dad was teaching us how to toughen up. Once, after Cameron and I accidentally got poison ivy all over our bodies and then finally recovered, Cameron's dad advised us to go outside and roll around in it again so that we could become immune. So we did. Instead of immunity, we got the same result as the first time. As far as his dad was concerned, if we got bucked off the horse, we certainly weren't going to cry about it, and you better believe we were getting back on to finish the job. His mom was equally frank, and I loved and respected both of them.

Cameron wasn't the only one with formidable parents. While my dad taught by example, my mom was intimidating and demanded respect. One day, when she'd discovered that Cameron and I had skipped school to go to a restaurant with some girls, she marched right in there and pulled us out from under the table, where we were hiding. Digging her long fingernails into both of us, she dragged us out of the restaurant by our ears. At the time, we were eighteen years old, over six feet tall, muscular, and tough. She was petite—five feet, five inches at her tallest. It was a toss-up who scared us more—my parents or Cameron's. What we didn't understand at the time was that their tough love was teaching us accountability, hard work, and discipline.

When Cameron and I first met, I could immediately sense that he was different. He didn't care if he was popular and certainly didn't seek out certain friends. He accepted anyone and didn't worry about where they fit in the junior high food chain, or even where he did. Fearless and always challenging the status quo, he was one of the first kids who introduced himself to me after I moved from Colorado. Not too long after that, whenever we were together, mischief was not far behind. He was the Butch Cassidy to my Sundance Kid, and we seemed to always be on the run. Whether toilet papering, snow balling, hunting deer, pulling pranks around town, camping, shooting, catching fish, or just enjoying the outdoors, whatever storm we chased, we chased it together.

I first smelled a "stink bomb" when I was walking to class one morning during my seventh-grade year. Not knowing what caused this foul odor but witnessing the instant reaction it made in the hallway, I was immediately intrigued. What was once a busy gathering of kids became a ghost town in seconds. It was as if the hall were quarantined—every possible route around it was made from necessity. As my peers ran away from the foul odor, I moved quickly toward it. This was the ultimate prank. Leaving no evidence behind, it was virtually undetectable. Out of the hundreds of kids walking up and down the hallway, no one knew who perpetrated the stink bomb. If someone could harness this rotten-egg power, I needed to know how.

After doing some detective work, I soon zeroed in on who the culprit might be: an older ninth grader wearing a look of giddiness was watching everyone scatter. During that week, I made a point of finding the boy and his accomplices and getting some more information.

Once I located them, I decided to play to their egos: "That wa-was hilarious today in the hallway," I stuttered. "I would never dare d-d-do something like that. You have to be a tough dude to puuu-pull something like that off."

Once they knew I was an admirer, it was amazing how quickly they opened up about where they had gotten their arsenal of magical items.

The stink bombs, I had discovered, could be purchased at a little hole-in-the-wall shop we locals simply referred to as The Basement.

I met up with Cameron after school, and we didn't waste any time as we walked downtown to The Basement to grab ourselves a case of stink bombs. They were packaged in little glass vials; we only needed to throw the stink bombs hard enough on the ground for them to break. After we understood how to use them, we came up with our plan of action.

Blending in with the crowd of students walking to and from class one morning, Cameron and I clutched our binders close to our chests while on opposite ends of the hallway. With a silent nod to each other, we stealthily reached inside our binders, slipping out the precious vials with sweaty fingers. Gripping them tightly, we waited as more and more students came out of their classes and funneled into the hall, providing the perfect cover. First Cameron threw down his vial, the noise in the hallway masking the sound of it hitting the floor. Patiently I waited for my turn. As students began to run toward me, I unleashed my vial, effectively trapping anyone trying to get away from the smell.

The more I unleashed the stink bombs, the more the suspicion was raised on a handful of proud ninth graders who had talked too much to a harmless seventh-grade admirer. I had the perfect diversion, and it worked every time.

By the time Cameron and I got to high school, we had grown a lot physically. Unfortunately, maturity and wisdom were still something that we were learning.

In my youth, the battle with my natural tendencies was frequent. There were times I used that energy for good—serving the widows in my neighborhood, shoveling snow, or cutting grass—and times that I didn't, but God always allowed me to choose, just as He allowed me to learn from the consequences my negative choices always brought. Most of what I did could be deemed as harmless, but there were other times when I took it too far.

I'll always be grateful for one experience and the lesson I learned about repentance, restitution, and the kindness of strangers I had wronged.

My three friends alternated turns sitting in the passenger seat of my Chevy Blazer while I drove. It was a cool October night, and the four of us were having a sleepover at my friend Bryan's house. I had just turned sixteen and was the only one of us that had a license. When you're the first one in your friend group to get a driver's license, everyone wants to be entertained by your newfound freedom, so with your golden ticket planted proudly in your wallet, you happily accommodate.

We decided to go joyriding that night. Before we left, someone noticed a brand-new baseball bat in Bryan's bedroom and grabbed it.

It was late, and most people were in bed. Someone put in a hard rock CD, which immediately set our mood on the path of destruction. It wasn't long before someone noticed the bat we had brought along and suggested we hang out the window and see how many mailboxes we could hit.

Rolling down the passenger-seat window, I yelled, "Batter up!" before concluding with a "Hey, batter, batter, swing!" Each time I finished my mantra, whichever of my friends was in the front seat at the time wound up as I drove closer to the curb. With a powerful swing, they'd smash the mailbox so hard it went sailing off its platform, landing some ten to fifteen feet away. This went on for roughly a half hour. We destroyed mailboxes every few houses, like a game of whack-a-mole. After the excitement and endorphins wore off, it began to dawn on us what we were doing.

"Boy, that escalated quickly," my friend Drew said lamely.

Turning the music off, we were suddenly aware of what had just taken place. We felt stupid and remorseful for what we had allowed ourselves to do. We were also fearful that we'd get caught, perhaps sensing that eventually this would catch up to us sooner rather than later.

We drove back to Bryan's house. Once we arrived, two of my friends hopped out of the car while Drew and I decided to go grab an early-morning breakfast at Dee's Restaurant. By this time, it was around two in the morning. Drew, who was a ninth grader at the time, asked me if he could drive my car. Jokingly I said, "You can't handle a stick shift."

"I can drive a stick in my sleep," Drew responded confidently.

It never occurred to me not to let him drive. So I pulled over. Drew hopped into the driver's seat, and with a massive grinding of the gears, confirming my suspicions, he took off swerving down the road while I buckled up.

It only took about half a block for blue and red lights to begin flashing in the rearview mirror.

"Hurry! Pull over and change seats with me!" I demanded.

As we fumbled to move past each other, a large spotlight shone through the back of my car. Looking down at the floor mat in front of Drew, I noticed the smashed bat covered in paint chips lying there.

"Hide the bat!" I nervously yelled.

Drew swiftly grabbed the bat before moving from the front seat to the back seat, where I had a blanket. Shoving the bat underneath the blanket, Drew hopped back into the front, all while the spotlight remained poised on our deeds.

Terrified, we waited for the cop to approach our car. As minutes began to pass, our hearts sank when one cop car after another drove up and parked around us. It wasn't long before this sleepy little street became abuzz with five police cars lining it, all shining their lights on us. One by one, lights began to flip on in the houses lining the street.

Finally, two cops got out of their car and slowly moved toward us. Rolling down my window, I tried to play it cool.

"Good morning, officer," I said.

"Boys, it's awfully late to be out driving," the officer replied. "Also, you seem to be struggling to stay in your own lane." Using his flashlight to light up my front seat, he asked, "Who else is in there with you?"

Trying to keep my voice steady, I replied, "This is my friend Drew."

"Boys, I'm going to need to search your car," the officer responded. "We've had calls throughout the neighborhood that somebody has been bashing mailboxes. And I saw your friend hide what looked like a baseball bat in the back seat of your car after you pulled over." He paused. "You're going to get out of the car now, one at a time."

Looking at each other, we knew life had just ended for both of us. Before I got out of the car, I told Drew to tell the truth.

After divulging all, we were both handcuffed and put in the back of one of the cop cars. The officers then demanded we take them to every mailbox we had demolished that night.

After that, a detailed report of our destruction was written up, and then Drew and I were placed in separate vehicles and taken back to our homes. Our other two friends who chose not to go to Dee's were still playing video games at Bryan's house, thinking that nothing had happened. They were in for a rude awakening when they woke up the next morning.

As the officer driving the car I was in got closer to my house, my stomach turned to knots. We arrived at my house, and the officer opened my car door. After pulling me out of the car, he unlocked the handcuffs around my wrists and then grabbed my shoulder, guiding me to the front door.

"My parents are going to kill me!" I sadly exclaimed.

The officer responded, "Son, that means you have good parents."

And he was right. I did.

All our parents went nuclear when they found out what we had done. My parents grounded me and took my driver's license away until I could prove that I could handle driving responsibly. Our parents then met together and determined that us boys would all dress up in our Sunday best. We would then find each person whose mailbox we had destroyed, tell them what we had done, and ask for forgiveness.

Walking up to each front door that day, I was bombarded by guilt. Under the cloak of darkness and hidden from others' watchful eyes, we refused to see the people beyond the mailboxes. Now in the light of day and face to face with the owners of the properties we had vandalized, I wanted nothing more than to be forgiven by those I had mistreated. Praying inwardly for forgiveness and mercy—both from the homeowners and our Heavenly Father—when each person opened the door, we explained to them what we had done and how we were going to make it right; our next few paychecks from each of our jobs would go toward purchasing new mailboxes.

Not a single homeowner yelled at us or pressed charges. Each of them understood that this was a valuable teaching experience, and they graciously allowed us to learn. It is amazing the power the forgiver holds in their hearts and in their hands. Being able to forgive gives a person seeking forgiveness the ability to move on. Equally important, that gift is then given to the forgiver as well.

Because these homeowners had acted out of love and my parents had made me accountable for what I had done, I saw the other side of my storm-chasing ways. I hated how I'd felt after the mailbox incident and realized that my life could go one of two ways, depending on if I learned to bridle some of my impulses.

I began to heed God's gentle breeze of whispered warnings to avoid chasing storms. I still made mistakes and continued to learn from them. Along the way I discovered that there is no limit to God's love for us. He not only gives us time to make and learn from mistakes here in mortality, but He also provides safe shelter from the storm if we so choose it. A loving and patient Savior will always show us another path, allowing us at any time to change direction and run toward Him.

As I neared the end of my senior year, I began to turn more and more toward my Savior and further from my old habits. Unbeknownst to me, my Heavenly Father was guiding me and teaching me invaluable lessons during the years of my youth. He knew a colossal storm was headed straight for me in the form of massive challenges and another disability. A category five in nature, this new storm would never let up and would often grow in ferocity. As I would sit in the midst of this tornado for the rest of my life, I would continue to learn to cling to my Savior's calming voice and find refuge in the eye of a storm that never ceased to rage.

Chapter 5

KING OF THE MOUNTAIN

"Dear Heavenly Father, I'm grateful that I have been born to such great parents. I'm grateful for the opportunity I have to serve as a missionary later this year, to be able to share Jesus Christ's teachings and to get closer to Thee. I'm grateful for Jessica and for our growing relationship. Please bless that no harm or danger will come to me or my family and our friends when we go to Lake Powell in July. I say these things humbly in the name of Thy Son, Jesus Christ, amen."

Five months before leaving to Lake Powell, Utah, for a vacation, these were the words of my prayers every night before I went to bed. I didn't want anything to go wrong this trip. For some reason I was scared that it would. It was almost as if I was waiting for the other shoe to drop. My life was going so well. I was the happiest I had been in years.

It was July of 1998, and I had just graduated from Bountiful High School a little over a month before. During my senior year, the effects of my traumatic brain injury and the challenges that came with it were less noticeable. My speech impediment was improving, and socially I was regaining confidence. Thanks to hours of persistent tutoring each night by my dad, I was also on track with what I should be learning for my age and grade. I finally felt like I was free again to be the Brandon I knew I was. I was passing most of my classes as well. Some teenagers and their parents might not be happy with average grades, but when I brought home my report card filled with Cs and Ds, my mom got out her Sharpie. Drawing a line over the top of my grades, she'd then replace them with As and Bs, knowing how hard we'd all worked to help me complete my homework assignments.

While I was improving mentally, physically I had found a more positive outlet for my energy and was excelling with rigorous weight lifting. There was a feeling of urgency I had while lifting that I couldn't explain. Images came to my mind of me working out my neck each time I went to the gym. They were so prevalent that I couldn't leave the gym until I had worked out my neck each day. This was odd; no one I knew focused on just that area—lats or shoulders, certainly, but I had never seen anyone solely work on their neck. I wasn't even sure how one would go about it. When I went to a trainer at the gym and expressed my desire, he raised his eyebrows and walked to the back room. Returning, he held out what appeared to be a medieval torture device. He handed it to me, jokingly saying, "Here it is, if you're into that kind of thing."

Holding the "head harness" out in front of me, I figured out how to put it on. An old-time-looking leather football helmet was placed on my head with two chains that hung just past my waist attached to either side. A large weight plate connected the two chains together. I would then move my head up and down slowly, which proved to be difficult and painful—it was obvious my neck was not as strong as the rest of my body.

Working out became religious for me. In the Bible, we read that our bodies are temples and gifts that God created for us. Because of this, we are told not to defile them. I wanted to make sure that I honored God's precious gift to me by becoming as healthy as possible.

My parents often reminded me while I was focusing on my physical body not to forget to work out my spiritual body. Because of this wise advice, I'd read from the scriptures when I awoke at 5:30 each morning for a half hour before leaving for the gym. There I would work out for an hour, change into my school clothes, and arrive at school by 7:30. Once school was out at 2:30, I'd go home and quickly change into my work clothes. From 3:00 to 7:00, I worked on getting my apprenticeship in commercial plumbing while building new houses. After work, I'd do homework until 10:00 and then head to bed and start the whole process over again the next morning. Weekends were a little bit more relaxed and usually consisted of dating and enjoying the outdoors. Fly fishing, hunting, and camping were my first loves, until I met another.

The first time I noticed Jessica was when my younger brother, Bronson, a junior in high school at the time, brought her home one night after they'd gone on a date. When I saw her, I knew that I had to get to know this pretty, curly-brown-haired girl who was two years younger than me. This made matters awkward. I asked Bronson if it would be okay if I took Jessica out on a date. He was a little surprised but said, "Sure, have at it."

After our first date, we were inseparable, hanging out almost every day after I got off school and home from work. At the same time that I was focused on Jessica, I was equally focused on my desire and plan to serve a church service mission later that fall. After waiting all the years of my youth, I was now finally grown up enough to go. The week before leaving for Lake Powell, I'd had a pre-mission physical to make sure I was ready to go anywhere in the world that I could potentially be called to serve.

"Brandon, you're as fit and strong as anyone I know," my doctor had joked during my physical. "You sure you're not applying for the Navy Seals?"

Laughing, I'd replied, "I'll first serve God and then country."

Once I returned from Lake Powell, I would then send in my physical assessment and other paperwork before looking forward to my mission assignment coming a couple weeks later in the mail.

When I arrived home after my physical, my little sister Bridgett, who had just turned eight, ran up to me and hugged my leg. I picked her up above my shoulders before giving her a big squeeze. I was her protector, role model, and big brother, and I loved her dearly.

"Are you going to miss me when I leave for two whole years?" I asked her with a smile. I knew that she would. To be honest, I would miss her too. A few months before, she had asked me if I would baptize her, since she was now old enough to make such a commitment. There were ten years of separation between us, and she'd always said that I was the one she wanted to perform this sacred ordinance. Looking back, it's clear to see that the Spirit whispered to Bridgett to give me this opportunity. It wouldn't be long after that opportunities like these would soon be physically impossible for me to perform. How grateful I am that I had this singular and sacred experience in my life. It was a privilege for me and something that I'll never forget.

What a wonderful and exciting time that year was for me. After graduating, I had total independence over the direction my life would take and where I was headed. All that was left was for me to fulfill my destiny of who I wanted to be and become that person moving forward.

When the long-anticipated day of our Lake Powell trip finally arrived, I was on cloud nine. I felt like a sight to behold wearing my form-fitting Hawaiian tank top that showed off my chiseled arms. Like a superhero only missing his cape, I drove to whisk Jessica away with me. She was just as excited as I was. Getting in the car, she hugged me while squeezing my arm. "Hey, handsome. It's so good to see you," she said.

Well before Jessica and I started dating, our moms knew each other. Best friends in high school, they now played tennis together at the local tennis club. Both of our families had met up that morning with our boats to make the five-hour drive down to Lake Powell.

With my mom driving and me sitting shotgun, I played DJ while Jessica sat in the back with her sister and her friend, jamming out to the music I picked. We sang and laughed the entire way down.

It seemed we arrived at the marina in no time. There we loaded our food and supplies for the week onto Jessica's parents' houseboat before launching out into the beautiful red-rock desert lake.

The houseboat took off on its two-hour drive, with our boats and Jet Skis following behind. We wasted little time once we arrived, enjoying the lake's warm water. Laughing and playing king of the mountain on the back of the houseboat, I'd gently toss the little kids into the water as they tried to throw me in. "Brandon, come chase us!" they called out, laughing hysterically and begging me to do it again.

Altogether there were twenty-three people on the houseboat, including my family of six, Jessica's family of ten, and another family of seven. That evening, all of us sat together watching the beautiful canopy of stars, in awe at all of God's creations shining back at us. A thousand miles from nowhere, everything was so clear. After months of anticipation, we were finally there.

Lightning flashed in the distance. It was the perfect night, made better by the fact that I was snuggled up to Jessica. I didn't want this approaching storm to ruin that. It was almost as if in the back of my mind I was aware that at any moment all of this could be taken from me. With our sleeping bags stretched over the deck, we lay talking about life. Smiling, I looked over at Jessica and asked, "Will you wait for me while I am gone and far away?" This wasn't the first time we talked about our possible future together. At that young age and experiencing love for the first time, we were confident in us.

Smiling back at me, she said, "Of course I will," before adding, "Will you write me?"

"Maybe," I joked. "I've got a lot of girls to write to."

Laughing, she reached for my hand as the thunderstorm drew nearer.

With each passing day, our families grew closer. Every afternoon, I spent some time teaching the little kids how to fish. They would impatiently wait for me to grab my fishing tackle and then drop whatever they were doing and run eagerly toward me once I'd picked it up. Not necessarily excited to fish but wanting to be with me, they took every opportunity to follow me around. I welcomed their company, not minding the endless hours spent showing them how to catch never-ending fish from the side of the bay that the house was secured to. I can still see the proud look on Bridgett's face and the sand stuck on her little legs. "That's so cool that your brother knows how to fish," one of her friends had said to her. Bragging, she had responded, "He takes me all the time."

These memories often play in my mind unwillingly, as if my body is trying desperately to find itself again. For me, the images are almost constant, like a movie stuck on repeat. It is a form of torture few people can understand.

On the sixth and second-to-last day of our trip, we left the houseboat and jumped onto two of our smaller boats. Traveling to the north end of the lake, we moved toward a place called Moki Canyon. This long, winding canyon featured jagged, vertical red-rock cliffs on both sides. We planned to dock at "Sand Mountain," a well-known spot located on the south end of the canyon.

As our boat turned a final corner, we suddenly saw the massive and daunting hill made of red sand shooting straight out of the water. Looking at it in awe, I pointed it out to Bridgett, who was seated on my lap. "You see those guys climbing to the top?" I asked.

She nodded.

"I'm going to do that!" I told her confidently.

"Look!" she said excitedly to the other kids, pointing out the people climbing up the hill as we docked our boat.

Three of my friends and I immediately hopped out of the boat and started to climb. We hadn't anticipated how hot the sand would be on our hands and feet as we moved up the steep hill. Consequently, we moved as quickly as possible. Once we got to the top, we buried our burning feet deep within the sand, finding spots where the sun's rays hadn't penetrated.

Like king of the mountain, I was on top of the world. Looking down at my parents, brother, and sisters below, I waved as they waved back from the bottom of the hill. Everyone was watching us on the dune. Some people were doing somersaults and flips on the way down. There was even a giant waterslide that someone had set up. I watched as a person on a snowboard passed below us. All around me people were laughing.

Well aware that I would be leaving on my service mission in a matter of months, I never had the desire to do something reckless. In fact, even though I didn't have a feeling that something was about to go terribly wrong, I still made a conscious decision to be careful, which was out of the norm for me, as the four of us began to run down the hill. With the roasting 102-degree temperature beating down on us, the soles of our bare feet were on fire once more. All thoughts were on getting to the water as quickly as possible.

We intended to start off slow, but it wasn't long before the steep grade of the hill, aided by gravity, began to move all of us along much quicker than we had wanted. Spaced about three feet apart from one another, we began running faster and faster to the point of uncontrollable speeds. Unable to stop myself, I could see the cool water getting closer as I continued to move at a pace faster than I had ever run. The water was now about ten yards away. I wanted nothing more than to dive into it, relieving myself of this hot desert sand. We were a blur as we zoomed past family and friends still watching some twenty-five feet away from us.

It was only a few more yards before I could safely dive head-first into the deep water that was beckoning to me. Suddenly, my legs got tripped up in the sand. I began to lose my balance. Like an Olympic sprinter leans over the finish line in one final and frantic push, I couldn't stop my runaway train. To this day, I often wish that somehow I would have known to let myself crash mid-hill, or even right at the water's edge. Far too much of my life since that day has been spent cursing myself, the trip to Lake Powell, the sand hill, and especially those plaguing ten seconds of time separating pre- and post-accident.

There is a quote given by Neal A. Maxwell that I often rehearse in my mind. It goes like this: "Indeed, if our souls had rings, as do trees, to measure the years of the greatest personal growth, the wide rings would likely reflect the years of greatest moisture—but from tears, not rainfall."[1]

Trying to correct my fall, with one last lunge I desperately tried to cover the ground my feet could not. It happened so quickly that for a moment I thought I had made the correct adjustment as I confidently dove headfirst to the side of my friends into the water.

They made it. I did not.

I first heard and then felt my neck violently snap. Feeling as though a bolt of lightning had just struck my body, I forcefully bounced off the shallow sandbank that I had hit. So powerful was the impact that it caused my lifeless but still conscious body to flip 360 degrees up and out of the water before slamming face down some six feet away into the lake.

A gut-chilling cry that I still hear to this day erupted from my mother, hauntingly reverberating through the canyon walls.

"He's dead! He's dead!" she screamed.

Her screams were followed by my father's cries: "Someone grab him! He's drowning!"

As I opened my eyes, I found myself looking downward into the depths of the lake. I was sinking. There was no pain, no feeling, no movement. Instantly, I was aware that I had broken my neck.

---

1. Neal A. Maxwell, "Thanks Be to God," *Ensign*, July 1982, 51.

There is no way I'm paralyzed! I kept thinking. *My life cannot end like this.*

A barrage of noises assaulted my ears. I could pick out individual voices: my mother's cries, my dad swimming urgently toward me, and the children's voices. I clearly remember thinking that these had to be the saddest sounds I would ever hear and the most heartbreaking send-off someone could possibly experience as they sunk to their death. I knew I was drowning, and I was convinced I would not live through this experience. Hearing everyone's reactions broke me in two. In absolute dismay, with all I was hearing, feeling, thinking, and seeing, I pled with my Father in Heaven to save me.

Urgently, I tried to move my legs and my arms, but to no avail. Holding my breath and quickly running out of air, I continued to sink into the darkness. Shaking my head back and forth repeatedly, I let everyone know I was still alive. My friend Ryan, who was the closest to me, swam as quickly as he could. As he reached my body, he flipped me over, and I gasped for air. My dad arrived shortly after. As he was cradling me in his arms, I said, "Dad, what happened? I think I just died!" His face pale and obviously in shock, he and Ryan pulled my immobile body through the water closer to the shore. There they pushed the sand away, creating a pocket for my head and shoulders to rest on. Gently they laid my head down in the sand while the rest of my body remained floating in the water, to help reduce the swelling and to keep me cool.

My dad yelled forcefully for the increasingly growing crowd not to touch me, afraid the slightest touch would inflict more damage. My mom remained frozen to the spot in the boat where she had seen me dive.

"Brandon, can you move your legs or arms?!" my dad asked, horrified.

"No," I responded in shock, my mind refusing to let reality enter.

On the second-largest man-made reservoir in the United States, with two thousand miles of shoreline, this was a worst-case scenario for a severe trauma. We were greatly in need of divine assistance. Praying, we were left waiting for someone to come while trying to comprehend the horrible predicament we were in. This beautiful, secluded lake had now become the trap that separated us from help. None of us had any way to reach out for assistance. There was no cell phone service, and the closest landline was at the marina, hours away. Internally, I pleaded with my Heavenly Father for a miracle. Looking at my dad, I said, "This is really bad. I need a blessing now!" Both of us knew the power of blessings. It was a little over six years before that I had needed another life-saving blessing. Now, here we were again.

By the time the blessing was over, all my family and friends were by my side, as well as bystanders who had witnessed the accident. Miraculously, two of those bystanders were ER doctors, one of many answers to our prayers that day. One grabbed my neck and held it in place, while the other yelled for someone to grab him a pen. With a black marker now in hand, the man began to pinch my body, each time asking me if I could feel the pain. Everyone's eyes were glued to my face, waiting to hear the only answer that could make everything okay. I wanted nothing more than to respond "yes," and I even contemplated saying it just to erase the looks on the faces of the people I loved, revealing to me the awful truth that I was not prepared to acknowledge.

Staring up at the sky, I focused on no one but the one being that I knew could heal me. Praying inwardly once again, I begged for feeling to come back to my body. At the same time,

I was aware that as I kept responding "no" to the question "Can you feel that?" the doctor would draw a large black line across my body. Like a ladder, line after line moved progressively higher up my frame, as if the cruelest human were heartlessly revealing that I had just become useless in front of my family, my girlfriend, strangers, my friends, and the entire world.

In front of all our eyes, my body was disappearing at reckless speeds as literal slashes were being drawn through my mobility.

First slash—my legs. *Running, hiking, fishing, skiing, climbing, driving, my mission.*

Second slash—my waist. *My girlfriend, a wife? Kids? My pride.*

Not only marking my body but also permanently changing my life, the black lines continued.

Third slash—my stomach. *My six pack, my stability, my bowels . . . my dignity.*

Heavenly Father, please! I pleaded. *Leave me something!*

My chest would follow suit, the black slash robbing more of my independence.

Lastly, my shoulders and neck. *Triceps, lats, biceps, the gym.* All my muscle lay in a pointless heap.

Tears sprang to my eyes as I thought, *Dear God, I've lost everything.*

I kept trying to reassure everyone that I was okay, knowing inside that I was anything but, while impatiently waiting for the coast guard to arrive.

Right before I had run down the sand hill, there had been a family passing by the area. They had intended to stay in another canyon during that week, but they had felt an overwhelming urge to stay in Moki Canyon instead. On the last day of their trip, as they drove from the canyon, they would suddenly stop their boat, both the husband and the wife having a strong impression to watch me run down the mountain. As they observed the tragic events unfold from a distance, they would be the ones to radio for help with a high-powered CB radio, newly purchased before their trip.

The family would call to us from the water, telling us that help was on the way before offering a prayer in our behalf. Eighteen years later, I would discover that these weren't just onlookers, but they were extended family members from my grandpa's sister's side that happened to be there. I do not doubt that God, in His infinite wisdom, choreographed the help I would need to be there in the moment I needed it.

The miracles did not stop there either. There are only two patrol boats on Lake Powell's waters that carry steroid shots used to reduce swelling from physical accidents such as mine. To my family's astonishment, one of these patrol boats was only thirty-five minutes away, and the other was eight hours away. If the boat had been more than a few hours away, I would have died when the swelling reached my trachea, or at the very least been dependent upon a ventilator for the rest of my days.

Once the boat arrived, Life Flight was immediately notified before the steroids were quickly injected into my blood stream, stopping my neck from further swelling. My mom and Jessica held my hands. No matter how hard I willed my fingers to respond, they only lay limp and lifeless. This beautiful, magnificently strong body that I could easily move and lift 350-pound objects with was not even able to swat away the flies landing on my face.

As the shock began to wear off, my neck started to hurt a great deal, a stark contrast to the eeriness of not feeling the water as it lapped against my body. It was a haunting experience, being present but only seeing what I should have been feeling.

One of the longest hours of my life passed before Life Flight finally arrived on the scene. I was hoping that I could take my mom with me, but because hot air within the canyon was already making it difficult to fly out, no extra weight could be added to the helicopter.

My mom and Jessica both kissed me on my cheek and told me, "We'll be right behind you." My dad, brother, and sisters quickly hugged me. "We love you, Brandon," they each told me. "We'll be praying for you and will be with you as soon as possible."

As I was loaded into the helicopter on a stretcher, out of the corner of my eye, I could just see out the window as we took off. I was unable to wave good-bye or even comprehend what in the world was happening. Staring at my family and friends below, I felt like I hadn't just said a temporary goodbye. Realization hit me full force that it wasn't temporary; I had literally just lifted off the ground and left my old life lying there.

An hour went by before we landed on the helipad of a small public airport in a little southern Utah town. Still another hour would pass as we waited for a medical jet to pick me up and fly me to Salt Lake City airport.

Once in the jet, I felt completely alone. All at once, depression, darkness, and emotion overwhelmed me. I began to fall into a dark pit of despair, knowing my life could not possibly get any worse than it was in that moment. No sooner had I felt this darkness within me than a bright flash struck the airplane, followed by a loud crack. One of the nurses jumped, exclaiming, "Oh, wow, that was scary!"

Pulled back from my darkness, I asked, "What in the world was that?"

Surprised, the nurse replied, "The airplane was just struck by lightning!"

I wondered if with one great flash of light God had literally snapped me out of the dark. I realized it's probably not wise to imagine that my life could not get any worse, at least until I was safely on the ground. There would be plenty of time for imagining the worst in the days, weeks, and months to come, as reality would become far worse than I ever could have conjured.

My mind turned to the memories of all the prayers I had uttered over and over again for five months before leaving to Lake Powell. Only this time I knew the outcome of the trip, and I was angry with God.

I asked You to protect me so I could serve You! I only wanted to serve You! Wasn't that a good desire?! Wasn't that what You wanted from me? And now, how can I do that when I can't even move or take care of myself? How could You do this to me?!

Among a bombardment of other thoughts, I lay wondering how I could possibly be of use in this life.

Six years before this accident, I would lose part of my brain capacity. Now, just getting back to who I was, I would lose my body.

It would be years before I would realize that I *would* serve a service mission for my Father in Heaven, though different than I could've ever imagined. It would begin that day and would never end as I gradually understood that I had not been chosen to survive, but called to live.

Chapter 6

EBENEZER

The hospital staff was waiting for me when I arrived. As I entered the emergency room doors, I was immediately rushed to surgery. A surgeon came over to my side and introduced himself. I looked him straight in the eye before saying, "Doc, you're going to fix this, right?"

The doctor's face was sober when he responded, "Brandon, there is no fixing this."

I can still recall the uncontrollable tears as they put me under anesthesia, along with one final thought, *Please, God, if I am really going to be paralyzed, please don't let me wake up.*

Little did I know that as my family made the five-hour drive back from Lake Powell, they would stop every couple of hours to pray when it became too difficult to keep driving. Knowing how cruel a life without legs would be for one as active as me, they would offer prayers containing the same plea as my own.

It was night, and I was all alone in the God-forsaken intensive care unit. It had been four days since I broke my neck and was told by the doctors that I was a C-5 quadriplegic. The surgeons had found a miniscule bruise located on a single nerve inside my spinal column. The contusion was no bigger than a piece of pencil lead.

The idea that this one tiny nerve had sustained damage as inconsequential in size as pencil lead and was preventing my entire body from moving again was unfathomable. How was that possible? In a world where science is advanced enough that skin can be regenerated, bone fragments can be rebuilt, fingers can be reattached, and organs can be transplanted, it was not conceivable to me that the cells in the spinal cord simply cannot repair themselves. I struggled to accept it. The idea that nothing could be done for a tiny bruise and that paralysis would not only be my diagnosis but also my destiny was infuriating.

I lay in bed wanting to run away from this living nightmare. I looked in sadness at my body that just a few days ago I controlled. Now it held me captive, physically trapped from the inside. My spirit, as hard as it tried, could not move it. My thoughts were quickly sinking toward endless despair. My only companions were the constant flashing lights and beeping of my vital monitors mixed with the rushing noise of oxygen being pushed through a tube in my mouth. I was in my darkest moment, dependent upon these medical devices and the nurses to keep me physically alive, while relying on my Savior to keep me spiritually present. As tears rolled down my cheeks, two questions plagued my mind.

Will I live through this?

Do I want to live through this?

Unable to sing out loud, with lungs too weak to breathe on their own, I mouthed that night the words to the song "Come, Thou Fount of Every Blessing":

> Come, Thou Fount of every blessing,
> Tune my heart to sing Thy grace;
> Streams of mercy, never ceasing,
> Call for songs of loudest praise.
> Teach me some melodious sonnet,
> Sung by flaming tongues above. . . .
>
> Here I raise my Ebenezer;
> Here by Thy great help I've come;
> And I hope, by Thy good pleasure,
> Safely to arrive at home.
> Let Thy goodness, like a fetter,
> Bind my wandering heart to Thee.
> Prone to wander, Lord, I feel it,
> Prone to leave the God I love;
> Here's my heart, O take and seal it,
> Seal it for Thy courts above.[2]

My mind reflected on the word "Ebenezer." I recalled many times while hiking seeing stacks of rocks placed one on top of another to form a type of tower. I would discover that these creations are often referred to as Ebenezers, the word meaning "stone of help." Hikers place these monumental stones at the top of a trail as their symbol that they have made it.

That night, as I lay in the hospital bed, I had never been faced with such an enormous dilemma. Overcome with anger, I realized for the first time in my life that my heart was "prone to wander" just as much as anyone else's. When my body could move, my heart was steadfast and fixed on my Savior. Now that

---

2. Robert Robinson, "Come, Thou Fount of Every Blessing," 1757.

I could not move, it was amazing to me how quickly my heart contemplated wandering to a place of darkness I never would've considered going before. I knew I had to make a decision in that moment. Choosing to sing that song was not an accident. I was fully aware that the Lord would help me through this, and at the same time I knew He was not going to change it. I wanted Him and especially myself to know that I was choosing to raise my Ebenezer to Him regardless of any outcome. This defining moment would set the tone for what my life would look like from then on. This would be the moment I chose to forever rely on Jesus Christ.

> God grant me the serenity to accept
>   the things I cannot change,
> Courage to change the things I can,
> And wisdom to know the difference.[3]

Even though I had made the decision not to wander from God, I would still struggle immensely with what lay ahead. Making that choice was not a singular event, but rather it was something I had to choose every living moment.

The first two weeks in the ICU recovering from neck surgery were a blur. I was on strict supervision by the doctors while my body adjusted to being completely paralyzed. For whatever effort my body made to conform, my mind would not comply. Waking up was a complete nightmare. Opening my eyes and looking at my immobile body was incredibly discouraging. I was a prisoner, but I had committed no crime. Sleeping was my escape. Closing my eyes, I'd pray for dreams in which I could

---

3. Reinhold Niebuhr, "Serenity Prayer," 1951.

run, jump, and be free. Reality was my nightmare. Dreaming was my relief.

It felt as if the joys of adulthood were ruthlessly stolen from me as I became a newborn again, completely dependent on adults to perform the necessities of life. But a newborn knows no shame or loss of dignity. Inevitably, they progress, move forward, and learn to do things on their own, while I could not feed myself, go to the bathroom, shower, get dressed, comb my hair, brush my teeth, get out of bed, roll over, and so many other things I'd taken for granted. I would be brutally reminded of this again and again as a body that no longer belonged to me refused to move.

For an eighteen-year-old boy, my female nurses were another humbling reminder that there would be many things I would never do again independently. Even that small act of having women close to my age undress me peeled back my pride one layer of clothing at a time.

The news of my accident quickly spread throughout my community. It seemed everyone came together in love and prayer for my well-being. My family was well loved in our large circle of friends and neighbors, and so was I. Even though I had my rebellious times, I always served in and around my neighborhood and in church, trying to treat everyone with love and respect. Soon many personal and family friends would come to visit me in the hospital.

People wanted so badly to give us hope. They'd come into my hospital room night after night and day after day, telling me I would walk again. "Just have faith, Brandon," they'd all say. They meant well, but it became incredibly overwhelming to me. I believed I would walk again more than any of them.

The constant and confident "I just know you are going to walk" began to do more harm than good, often resulting in me wondering, *If I don't walk again, will that mean they don't think I have faith? And, worse, if I don't walk again, will that affect their faith?*

But there was something that I understood despite their hopes for me: there is a fine line between faith and reality. All the faith in the world could not make me walk again if it was not God's will for me. I would soon come to realize that it takes far more faith to accept God's will for you than to ask Him to change it.

It finally got to the point where I needed to find my own foundation of faith and cope without the encouragement of others. It was then that we had to limit the time visitors could come. Regardless of what they hoped or thought, the reality was that my faith had nothing to do with me walking again and everything to do with how I would handle this trial from here on out.

Overwhelmed by the sheer number of visitors and feeling like I was losing myself, I turned to my mom with legitimate fear and concern. "I have nothing to show them," I said, completely dejected. "I'm paralyzed."

Immediately, she grabbed my hand and placed it over my heart. "No," she said firmly but lovingly, "you're not paralyzed. You're Brandon!"

From the wisdom of a loving mother, I understood that I was still me. I wasn't going to let my circumstance define me. If anything, it would refine me and turn me into a better version of the person I currently was. I relied on the strength of my loving parents as well as my faith in God to keep me sane those first few weeks.

Friends and visitors came often to say hello. In the corner of my hospital room, my family set up a remembrance book, where my visitors could write down a few words of encouragement along with their names. Lying in bed, out of the corner of my eye, I'd watch them quietly walk into my room with tears in their eyes as they wrote in my book.

Trying to lighten the mood, I'd often remark, "Hey, this isn't a funeral! I'm not dead yet, but if you keep writing and crying about it, you may just kill me." They'd laugh, and the ice of discomfort would crack slightly as we all tried to find something to talk about besides the elephant in the room.

One day, when some of my guy friends were visiting, I had a brilliant idea. Jessica, who was visiting me daily, would often scroll through the pages of past visitors and read their comments and well wishes. I decided to pay her back for her kindness by playing a practical joke on her. Talking to my friends one day, I said, "Hey guys, let's cook the books. Every time you come in, you're going to sign a different girl's name and write sweet nothings about me."

They immediately loved the idea. Needless to say, there are a lot of made-up girls' names giving me glowing reviews in my book. It was hilarious watching Jessica trying to figure out who these girls were and where they came from.

By this time, weeks had passed with no miraculous recovery—although there were other miracles. My brother, Bronson, was the first to notice that just a couple weeks after my accident, I seemed to be sharper and wittier than I had been in years. I noticed it as well. Amazingly, speaking was no longer a struggle for me. I truly believe that all lasting effects of my TBI were taken from me after I became paralyzed, as if the Lord, in His infinite mercy, decided to rid me of one huge trial as I began to battle another.

While mentally feeling keener than I had felt in many years, physically I was making little to no progress. I'd do exercises in bed with elastic bands as my arms slowly started to move again.

Roughly 20 percent of my muscles worked, which was limited to my biceps and shoulders. The rest of the muscles in my body were of no use whatsoever.

Eventually, I was transferred to the neuro-rehabilitation unit to begin my rehab process. Once I was in my new room, the nurses rolled a wheelchair in and left it there, as if to say, "Yeah, this is what you're going to be in your whole life. You might as well get used to it."

Rolling my eyes in disgust, I thought, *There is no way I'm spending my life in that wheelchair. I will beat the odds and walk again.* I was more than a little anxious to get the process of recovery started.

It took two strong guys to lift me out of bed and into the old, rickety wheelchair I called "the Cadillac," on account of it being huge, heavy, and ugly. Without muscle tone from your lower body, it's difficult for your body to pump blood to your heart. Consequently, I passed out three times just sitting in the chair. By the time I could sit in the chair without incident, a half hour had already passed. Bronson steered the Cadillac with me in it toward the therapy room. Unbeknownst to me, my dad had sat in a wheelchair in that very room days earlier. For two hours, he sat sobbing while trying to comprehend what my life would now look like. His outlook was that of a father who had lived years longer than me and had seen realities that I had yet to experience. I, on the other hand, was not prepared for what lay ahead.

I arrived to rehab in my Hawaiian tank top, with a pre-accident mindset that matched my outfit. I was ready to work out at the gym, just as I had done daily before my spinal cord injury. My excitement quickly unraveled when I saw the demographic of this gym. The patrons weren't quite what I was used to. I told Bronson to stop pushing me.

"What is this, a geriatrics rehab facility?" I asked him, confused. "You sure I'm at the right rehab?"

My neck was still in a neck brace, limiting my ability to look around, but I was sure we were lost. Bronson, knowing we were in the right place but not wanting to be the bearer of bad news, rolled me over to the nurse's station so I could ask. A nurse obviously used to speaking to those of a more mature and senile mind looked at me like I was four years old. "Yes, honey," she said to me sweetly and with feigned excitement, the kind you'd use when taking a kid to the dentist or a dog to the vet. "This is it!"

Suddenly, to the left of me, an old man in a wheelchair raced by. By "old man," I mean he was probably in his fifties, but since I was eighteen at the time, I figured he was ancient. He took one look at me before saying, "You wanna race?!" Zooming off, he looked back at me, challenging me to follow him, before popping a wheelie.

In disgust and embarrassment, I jokingly fired back, "Hey, aren't I supposed to be helping you cross the street?" For someone looking at my upper body, I still appeared to be strong and capable; he'd probably figured I was a paraplegic like him. Still, he had lit a fire within me. Seeing this role reversal happening right before my eyes, I attempted to push my Cadillac to catch up to this speedster, only to find I could push just a couple times before completely exhausting myself. I knew then that this gym would not be like any other I had experienced previously.

My therapy started every morning, Monday through Friday, at 9:00 a.m. and did not end until 3:30 p.m. All of it centered on me becoming more independent in a wheelchair. This made me furious. My ending goal had nothing to do with this stupid chair. Why base my time and exercises on that? We should have been doing things that focused on me walking again! I felt like so much time was being wasted.

My first few weeks in therapy were eye-opening on so many levels. What stood out the most, however, was how people reacted to their various challenges. I wasn't the only one trying to overcome a life-changing and debilitating disability. Many of the patients were older and going through hip and knee replacements, severe strokes, brain tumors, cancers, and other conditions. I could usually tell by the lack of light in their eyes when they had given up on themselves. I remember thinking what a terrible thing it must be to lose control of one's attitude, the one thing all of us in that room could still control.

Fear and faith cannot coexist. I saw firsthand that when we allow our circumstances to dictate how we feel and who we are, we may instantly become bitter. On the flip side, if we can learn to adapt to our challenges by focusing on what we *can* control in life, our attitudes and actions become better.

I heard people complain daily about things that I wished I could do. While they spoke of the pain they felt when they walked, I'd think to myself, *How about the pain you feel when you* can't *walk?* In therapy I wasn't just learning to work with my new body; I was being schooled and taught while watching others what not to become. Whenever I found myself getting depressed, I would often repeat to myself, *You are not going to be a sad case in a wheelchair. You're Brandon, a child of a God who loves you.*

Still determined not to let my suffering paralyze me inside, I began to embrace the *P* word. I wasn't going to let go of my goal of complete recovery and walking again. I knew that it was going to happen either in this life or in the next life, but I wasn't going to sit idly by waiting for it to happen either. I had to learn how to press forward successfully in a wheelchair if I was going to have a healthy and productive life, even if that life had me permanently sitting down.

Up to that point, in every therapy I'd had, I'd harbored a personal vendetta against the wheelchair, not understanding it was the very thing that could bring me physical freedom. I was so determined to get out of it that I didn't recognize that being in it brought me the independence I desired. Once I accepted this reality, I was finally ready to press forward with everything I had left physically. With faith intact, I desperately hoped that somehow it would all work out.

I started to learn how to operate my wheelchair. Soon I gained confidence in being able to maneuver my new four-wheeled friend.

On my second-to-last week of my seventy-two-day hospital stay, my therapist told me that I was going to learn how to go downhill in the wheelchair. My first impression was, "Sweet!" It had been a while since I had felt the cool breeze and exhilaration that came from running, which I dearly missed. I needed some excitement and to feel the air brush up against my skin. I needed to feel alive. I needed speed. After a month of pushing slowly in my wheelchair, I still couldn't beat "old man" Jim from therapy off the line. He was too fast. I was too slow. He had full upper body mobility while I had limited. I needed a change of pace, and quick.

Excited, I looked at my wheelchair in anticipation. I envisioned myself letting the wheelchair run free while I easily and expertly maneuvered it, like a jockey on a thoroughbred. I was disappointed, however, when I found out that I wasn't going to be going down the large hill outside the hospital. Instead, I would be going down a short ramp between the cafeteria and X-ray department. One could hardly classify the ramp as a speed bump, let alone a hill. My therapist cautioned me that going downhill is actually harder than going uphill, while reminding me where my brakes were in the event that I lost control. Her words went in one ear and out the other; I was too excited to listen.

As she let go of my wheelchair, I suddenly felt the rush I had yearned for. However, it was quickly replaced by a rush of panic as I realized I was completely out of control! It felt like I was going Mach two as I yelled for help while warning everyone in my path to move it or lose it! Even my therapist was screaming after she unsuccessfully tried to catch me. Clearly, I was in a situation that I could not control. I knew what to do in these types of situations, however. The key was to adapt. Instantly, I began to contemplate which body part I could do without. Obviously, it came down to the ones I couldn't feel. I didn't have strength to stop the wheelchair with my hands. I couldn't reach the brakes because my balance was all out of whack, and if I leaned forward, I would fall out of my chair. Since I had no feeling in my legs and feet, I thought, *Perfect! Those will serve as airbags!*

At the end of the ramp there suddenly appeared two huge steel elevator doors quickly approaching. I screamed out loud, "Open! Open! For the love of humanity, open!" I prayed not just for the elevator doors to open but that they would be jam packed with people inside who would cushion my impact. Unfortunately for me, the doors remained closed. My knees smacked hard as I slammed into the doors. It sounded like I had just hit one of those large Chinese cymbals that make a loud sound as they vibrate. *BOOOONNNNGGG.* The sound echoed throughout the basement of the hospital. The good news was that I couldn't feel my legs. The bad news was that I still couldn't feel my legs.

Slowly rolling myself away from the doors, I noticed I had left a calling card: an unmistakable impression of both my knees in the elevator doors. That was my first experience fully realizing how little feeling I had in my legs. I was immediately rushed to X-ray, and we discovered that nothing was seriously injured except my pride. Everyone on the unit and I had a good laugh about it.

As the weeks moved on, so seemingly positive was I amidst my disability that soon all four major TV news stations in Utah, as well as many newspapers, did a story on me. I tried to reflect what my mom had said to me, that I was still Brandon and that was never going to change. With my unbreakable faith in my loving Heavenly Father and knowledge that He had a plan for my life, I had nothing to fear, except fear.

One evening after rehab, my family and I were excited to see me on TV. That day, the local Channel 5 news team had done a story about my accident and how my faith in Jesus Christ and my positive attitude were helping me through my trial. I wanted to look good even if I was in wheelchair. I chose to wear my favorite Hawaiian tank top while they shot a video of me working out with my therapist. During my interview, I was asked how much my life had changed since breaking my neck. Hearing that question and seeing myself on TV later, I was immediately and suddenly unraveled. Instantly the darkness was back, as if it had been constantly near and waiting for any thought, any feeling, any image to allow itself passage within my soul.

Before seeing myself on TV, I had thought myself to still look as strong as I had three months prior. Somehow, I had completely forgotten that I had lost all my muscle. Although I could hear my voice and see my face, I did not recognize the emaciated frame. In complete and utter dismay, as if I had only just now realized the transformation that had taken place, I responded, dumbfounded, "My body! My muscles— it's all gone!" I had not realized what a paralyzed body looked like. In the blink of an eye, I had gone from 205

pounds, full of muscle, to 140, at best. That was the last time I wore my favorite tank top.

As I watched in utter dismay, the darkness taunted me. *Your body's never coming back either.*

It was in that moment that I realized there would be another burden that came with this disability—an almost constant struggle between the dark and the light. I would be on the front lines of this battle for the rest of my life. This was not a passive fight either; it was an all-out war. Beckoning me to lay down my weapons of faith and to give up, the darkness would scream at me that my trial was too hard, too big, and too constant. When I was at my weakest, the darkness would attack the hardest. Each day, it would take constant and deliberate effort to find the light again.

Chapter 7

REBUILDING

Imagine yourself as a living house. God comes in to rebuild that house. At first, perhaps, you can understand what He is doing. He is getting the drains right and stopping the leaks in the roof and so on; you knew that those jobs needed doing and so you are not surprised. But presently He starts knocking the house about in a way that hurts abominably and does not seem to make any sense. What on earth is He up to? The explanation is that He is building quite a different house from the one you thought of—throwing out a new wing here, putting on an extra floor there, running up towers, making courtyards. You thought you were being made into a decent little cottage: but He is building a palace. He intends to come and live in it Himself.[4]

—C. S. Lewis

Two years before my spinal cord injury, my mom began having an ominous feeling that she could not shake. In the back of her

---

4. C. S. Lewis, *Mere Christianity* (Macmillan Publishers, 1952).

mind, she sensed that plans needed to be drawn up to alter our house, making it wheelchair accessible. The first time it happened, it was just an odd thought. As the feeling persisted and grew in its urgency, she would no longer just feel that the house needed to be changed, but that eventually those modifications would be for me. Terrified, she only ever mentioned the feelings to my dad, and not often. Most of the time, she carried the worry inwardly.

Eventually, hoping to appease the thoughts, she drew up plans of a remodel, turning our two-story house into a rambler. Once finished, she convinced herself that the impressions weren't about me but instead centered on one day, a lifetime away, when she and my dad, peppered with age, would live out their remaining years in the house. That way the feelings could make sense to a mother's heart. It would be okay and maybe even natural for one of them by that time to need a wheelchair. Finishing the plans one day, she reached into the highest cupboard in our kitchen and slipped them into a far corner. In the back of her mind sat one last uneasy thought, until it became reality: *I hope I never have to pull these back out again.*

At the same time I was fighting my own battle, all of my family members were battling theirs. My sisters, Bridgett and Brittney, only eight and thirteen at the time, were often staying with neighbors, while Bronson, who was seventeen, was raising himself. All of them, feeling neglected and constantly scared, could not understand what was going on. My parents were at the hospital almost twenty-four seven. We had been told that whatever condition I was in after three months was what my life would look like forever. So desperate was I not to have this be my future that at times I would lie and say I felt some kind of movement. Everyone's hopes would then go back up, and we'd all start our emotional ordeal all over again.

At the time, my mom was only thirty-nine years old, my dad just forty-five. Not eating or sleeping, they were both constantly sick and exhausted and carried the perpetual guilt of not being able to function in their various roles as parents and providers. My mom would remark one night that she genuinely felt that her heart would stop at any moment and she'd die of a heart attack. When she did finally lie down to get some sleep, she'd hear the same thing whether in her dreams or reality: sounds of me running up and down the stairs over and over again would haunt her for years.

The happiness our family had accumulated over hours, days, weeks, and years together was taken in an instant. No one could laugh, smile, or live.

To complicate matters further, my dad had just changed insurance plans in the last week of July, right before we went to Lake Powell. With bills already beginning to pile up, our old provider would only cover the rest of July, while the new provider would label what had happened to me eight days previously as a pre-existing condition and refuse to pay any of it. My dad would shoulder the burden and spend the next several years dealing with the insurance company to get the hundreds of thousands of dollars paid.

On top of everything, there quickly came the looming feelings of living in a two-story house that was nowhere near handicapped accessible. While my dad tried to concentrate at work, feelings of me, the other kids, and whether we should rip our house apart or keep hoping for a miracle constantly occupied his thoughts.

Late one night, my dad was sitting alone in the garage, praying fervently to know what to do. The house had to be remodeled. I would be coming home soon, and too much time had already passed. In that moment, our friend, the bishop of our church, came over. Patting my dad on the back, he told him, "Whatever you are worried about, you need to move forward with this remodel and have faith that the Lord knows all your concerns and will provide."

With a head full of doubts and life now proving to him just how unpredictable and unfair it could be, he had to exercise a tremendous amount of faith, not only as a father but also as a provider, to move forward.

A kind architect in our neighborhood showed up at the house one day to show my parents a design he had done for a possible add-on, hoping it would help us move forward on the remodel. Thanking him, my mom reluctantly walked over to the cupboard she never wanted to open and pulled out the fateful design she had drawn up years before. Handing it to him, she explained. "Please use this."

I would not find out about the house plans she had drawn out years previously until after I was home from the hospital and those designs were well on their way to reality. Though she originally created them out of anxiety, one day she would come to understand that she had turned fear into faith that day. A mother full of worry for her son's uncertain and bleak future would sit down and consider that if this nightmare did in fact one day become my reality, she would make sure my new home was perfect for me. Long hallways for me to ride up and down. Windows strategically placed so that I might view the mountains I so loved but could no longer climb. The layout was meant not only to be functional but also to portray peace. I would need more than wide hallways and lowered countertops, something she somehow understood before any of this had happened.

As the remodeling began, one by one people came out of the woodwork. My dad still refers to them as the angels that always seemed to come whenever needed. Every night he would get home from work, head right to the garage, and begin work on the house until late into the morning. Inevitably, as he sat overwhelmed, he would feel a hand on his shoulder. "How can I help?" a neighbor would ask. "I had a feeling to come over. What do you need?" would become repetition reverently whispered in that garage, often after a humble prayer had been offered asking the Lord for help yet again.

This would go on until the house was complete. When footings needed to be dug, my dad, not knowing where to start and contemplating what to do, would be lost in thought just as my friend Cameron and his dad would show up with two backhoes. They would not stop there—using his connection to concrete, Cameron's dad would provide that next. A crew of friends would help with the framing too. Before my dad could even anticipate how they would pay for all the wire needed for the new electrical work, someone else was there, offering my father a huge bundle of leftover wire from a job they had been working on. Next, an attorney who lived nearby would instruct a drywall company that owed him ten thousand dollars to pay off their debt by doing our drywall.

It wasn't just people from the neighborhood that showed up either. Kids from my school in the same construction trade class that I had been in would come with my teachers and work on the house regularly. No one ever charged, and the constant stream of angels never ceased until the project was done.

Fundraisers, car washes, yard sales, golf tournaments, and many generous donations would provide the needed money to pay for materials as well as a new wheelchair-accessible van. The impact of my accident was far-reaching in our community and beyond—even little children were doing lemonade stands to help my family.

While people were working hard all around me to get things ready for my return home, I was hard at work trying to relearn a few simple tasks before I could be discharged. It took weeks of practicing to get my arms to make the controlled and precise movements to comb my hair, using a piece of Velcro strapped around my wrist and attached to the comb. With a lot of patience and many bad hair days, I finally mastered my goal. It was a big deal and gave me the motivation I needed to continue to press forward. Feeding myself took an additional four weeks.

Several times the nurses would leave food for me on a tray that sat above my lap before leaving the room. Whether they forgot I could not feed myself, were too busy to care, or were trying to motivate me, I don't know. Desperate to eat, I'd attempt to lob my hand at the plate. It would do little more than nudge the tray. My fingers were not able to obey my hungry stomach's demands. There was no way I could feed myself. Finally, I'd say, "To heck with it," and just face plant in the middle of my tray, eating my dinner as best I could.

Even though I had been in the hospital for almost three months and itching to get out, I was nervous about being discharged. When you become paralyzed, you're so busy fighting to survive and learning how to do so in the hospital that you don't think too much about what life will be like after. Once reality set in that I would soon leave, I began fighting like mad to quickly learn how to survive and live everyday life outside the hospital.

Although I was making progress, I wasn't anywhere near being independent. Outside the hospital doors, where handicap signs mark a few spots here and there, life is not made for people like me. I knew my survival was going to be terribly difficult. Left alone with these thoughts one day, I began to feel overwhelmed. I had to get away from my hospital room and the rehab unit to clear my mind. I needed to know what it felt like to be on my own, even if only for a short time. After rehab was finished, instead of returning to my room for dinner, and without my nurses' knowledge, I planned my great escape. Pushing myself slowly, but as fast as I could, I made my move toward the elevators. I had always wanted to explore this huge hospital, and I wasn't going to let this opportunity go by without trying.

Entering the elevators, I noted the generous supply of buttons to push. It was like a game show for me, as I waited to see what was behind each door when it opened. If I found the contents behind the door interesting, out I went. Rolling around, I'd take in all the sights and sounds.

To my surprise and satisfaction, I found four other elevators throughout the hospital that were virgin ground for me. I got so carried away that I quickly wore out my shoulders pushing my chair. Soon I could go no further. Noticing I was near the labor and delivery unit, I stopped to rest while looking at the cute little newborn babies through the window.

I was vaguely aware of the "Code yellow on T5. Code yellow on T5" that seemed to be paging throughout the hospital every five minutes. While resting and still gazing at the babies, I noticed a cute nurse walk by.

"Excuse me, what is a code yellow?" I asked her curiously.

"Code yellow means we have a missing patient," she replied, "and T5 means they're from the rehabilitation unit."

My eyes quickly widened. "Um, can you do me a favor?" I asked her, trying to stifle a laugh.

"Sure," she responded. "What do you need?"

"Can you tell them you found me and that I'll be pushing my way back?" I said.

When the nurse realized I was the missing patient, she laughed. "All right," she responded. "I'll let them know you're on your way."

I think I chuckled the entire way back to my room, before I began wondering if outside these hospital walls there is a code yellow when someone like me gets lost.

In those first few months, I prayed often and fervently to my Heavenly Father that some form of movement and feeling would come back into my lifeless body. Honestly, I still do. That may be surprising to some people, that after almost twenty years I still pray to walk again. I will always leave that light on for my independence, if God wills it, to come back in this life. Regardless, I have to have hope. Plus, I believe in miracles.

Slowly with time, some of my feeling did come back, albeit extremely dull and lackluster. Still, I was very excited at the prospect of any feeling returning to my body. I wanted to feel touch and the full beauty of it on my skin. The anticipation of that option was quickly replaced, however, when I did not feel what I wanted and instead began to experience nerve pain, extreme levels of pain so powerful that it can literally control my emotions and mind. It is excruciating. So horrid is nerve pain that some quadriplegics have elected to have surgery to completely detach their spinal cord, stopping any and all feeling completely, just to be relieved of this incessant torture. The fact that someone in my situation would be willing to sever all possibilities of walking again, when that hope is our primary focus, should give a little bit of understanding as to how horribly painful nerve pain can be. The irony that I had prayed and prayed to feel anything and nerve pain was the result only made my battle to push out the darkness harder.

I wanted so desperately to feel touch. As I was lying in my hospital bed, Jessica would often stand over it, grasping my hand and wrapping her fingers in between mine. Besides my loving family, she was most often by my side. I was constantly torn, thinking about telling the full truth about my pain and physical limitations to the one person I feared losing the most at the time. I knew my family would love me regardless, but deep down I knew that Jessica, like most sixteen-year-olds would be, was first in love with who I was physically and second with who I was inside. I wouldn't be honest if I didn't say it was how I felt as well. However, the care and concern she showed me during those months in the hospital was a great gift to me, and I cared about her deeply.

Two months after I had been discharged back to my home, Jessica would tell me a final goodbye. She would walk away, but I could not. I saw her everywhere I went: church functions, hanging out with mutual friends, and even passing on the street in front of my house.

The amount of pain I was feeling after that, on all levels, was incredible. It took a while for me to get over the heartbreak of losing my first love. Fortunately, I would find love again. Unfortunately, that would not be the last time I would lose it.

As we drove home on the last day of my hospital stay, we crossed into uncharted territory, hoping we could all journey this new path together without losing our lives and minds in the process.

While it is true that we came together in faith and love to try and slowly rebuild our family, we suffered together as well. Each of us battled our own personal and private hell. We fought not to burden one another, while recognizing that equal time was no longer something that was possible. I would take up the brunt of my parents' time, and my siblings would grow up far too fast. But our faith was strong, and we actively fought to stay a family unit. The first thing my parents were told after my accident was that 80 percent of marriages would not make it through what they were facing. Even though this was the wrong time and way to divulge such a devastating statistic, my parents vowed they would remain in the 20 percent. While it may be true that many families do not stay together after going through large-scale adversity, we chose to buck the status quo.

As we pulled up to the house, I was shocked at what I saw. The garage was completely torn down, as was the driveway. Until construction was complete, there was no wheelchair-accessible bedroom, bathroom, toilet, shower, or kitchen.

A long, thirty-foot plywood wheelchair ramp had been built over the front steps. It sloped downward until it reached the sidewalk. *Welcome Home* signs and banners were wrapped around the front porch of our house, waiting to greet me, and many of my friends and extended family members stood outside, holding balloons and signs of their own.

There are some moments in life when each of us has to fake like we're happy. This was definitely one of them. I was terrified of what I saw. Getting out of the car, I wondered how we were going to make this work, and I wasn't the only one. My parents were facing yet another mountain to climb, and each mountain seemed to be getting steeper.

I quickly found that "normal" would never exist again. In fact, the opposite was true. Being home was overwhelmingly difficult, and at times I yearned to go back to the hospital and live the remainder of my days there. Staying alive didn't seem that hard to me seventy-five days before, but now it would become my daily fight. In the hospital, machines alerted hospital staff when something was wrong. Nurses and doctors immediately filed into my room, bringing with them years of experience, training, and expertise. Not only that, but they had the appropriate equipment and supplies, things that were greatly lacking at home, making even the most menial tasks not just difficult, but almost impossible to perform.

Left to our own devices, suddenly necessary skills, like eating and going to the bathroom, became unbearable. Someone had to be with me at least every four hours for the rest of forever.

Though we trained in the hospital how to keep me alive at home, those first few years were humbling.

Until the remodel was complete, a makeshift bedroom would be set up for me in the small dining room next to the front door. It was just big enough for a twin bed and a wheelchair to fit in, and with no doors for privacy, my room was separated from the front hallway and those coming in and out of the house by a long shower curtain.

Because there were no accessible sinks for me to wheel underneath, my mom used a cooking bowl full of soap and water often to wash my hands and prevent infection. She also catheterized me and helped me with bowel care. Each day she or my dad dressed and undressed me and got me in and out of bed. Weekly, for the next year, my parents would drive me twenty-five minutes away, back to the hospital so I could shower in a vacant hospital room.

Every few hours nightly, and in addition to changing my catheter, my parents had to roll me back and forth on the bed so I didn't get any pressure sores on my skin from lying in the same position for too long.

Every time my bladder was full, I'd go through what's called dysreflexia, which would send my body into shock accompanied by a rapidly pounding heart. If not quickly relieved, it could lead to a massive heart attack or stroke. When this happened, my body would send warning signals to my heart that something was wrong.

It seemed that something was always wrong in those first couple of years.

One day, I called my mom, who had run out to show a client a house. In a panic, I pleaded over the phone. "Mom, can you please come home? My bladder feels so full!"

"I just cathed you two hours ago," my mom said, surprised. "How can you be full already?" Before I could answer her, she responded, "I'm showing a house thirty minutes away. I'll be right there."

By this time, my head was pounding. I didn't know which would rupture first, my bladder or my heart. I began to sob uncontrollably. This was no way to live a life, and no way for my parents to live theirs. While I waited in agony, I prayed to my Heavenly Father for life to somehow get easier for us and for us to have the strength to withstand our burdens for however long He'd allow.

By the time my mom got home, I was writhing in pain. She quickly helped relieve the pressure of a full bladder. Afterward, we both collapsed on the bed and cried. This wasn't a new emergency, nor was it the last time it would happen. This scenario repeated itself countless times. A mere three months previously, I had left my house as a physically independent man. I had returned as helpless as a baby. My parents would have to take care of me all over again—only this time, most things I would never learn to do on my own.

As God began to remodel my life as well as my spirit, I had to actively put trust in the Master Carpenter. He held the blueprints that I could not see. That trust would become my foundation in what would only be phase two in a massive remodel, turning me into so much more than I could have ever become on my own.

Chapter 8

ROCK BOTTOM AND HOLDING ON

With the house remodel now finished, I had my own beautiful wheelchair-accessible apartment. As the months went on, my body slowly got used to lying in bed without having to be rolled over. Eventually, I was also able to sleep through the night without having to have my catheter changed either. I finally became more mobile in my wheelchair, and a year later, I even learned how to catheterize myself. Still, even with these advancements, I was just barely holding on.

After my SCI, I was often asked to speak about my accident to various groups. One afternoon I was called by a church leader from a neighboring city, asking me to speak to a young adult group. I wasn't sure if I had much to offer, but this was a chance to serve, even if it wasn't walking door to door preaching the gospel, like I had wanted. I accepted this church leader's request and thanked him for the opportunity. A couple of weeks later, I addressed the young adults.

After I had finished talking to the group, the religious leader who had asked me to speak approached me. Patting me on the shoulder, he said, "You're amazing, Brandon! We're so blessed to have you here and grateful for the message you gave. It was perfect!" I thanked him again for the opportunity before he turned and walked away. It was then that I noticed a beautiful blond-haired girl walking up to the front of the room to shake my hand. We immediately made a connection and started talking back and forth about life. Out of the corner of my eye, I noticed the religious leader quickly making his way back over to me. Interrupting our conversation, he indicated to me that he was the father of the girl I was talking to.

I smiled at him and said, "You have a beautiful daughter."

Immediately his countenance changed. What before was praise and kindness toward me turned into a look of worry and concern. Sadly, the look was one I was becoming more and more accustomed to seeing. I clearly understood that he didn't want his daughter and me to continue our conversation. He feared, like they all did, that it could lead to her possibly dating a guy like me, a guy with a disability. Confirming my thoughts, he quickly pulled one of his friends over as a distraction before ushering his daughter away.

Later that evening, my brother was driving me back home. I was devastated. The feelings of peace that had surrounded me as I had spoken to the young adult group were now replaced with sadness. "Everybody praises me when they want me to speak," I lamented to Bronson, "but heaven forbid one of their daughters actually be interested in a guy like me." I shook my head. "Do you know what I am?" I asked rhetorically. "I am a man who volunteers, someone who keeps himself clean and worthy. I am respectful and complimentary. I am honest and caring. I am every father's dream," I said. "As long as I am standing." Emotion caught in my throat. "I am an asset turned liability."

"I can't hold on to a girlfriend, let alone a fishing pole!" I said to my dad, who had approached me with the idea of a fishing vacation to Ketchikan, Alaska, something the old Brandon would have loved to do. "I don't need another disappointment in my life!" I finished.

I had hit rock bottom. By now, most of my friends had left on their own missions or gone to college, and I was stuck at home. Dating girls had become painfully challenging. Trying my best to hide my disability in my relationships, I'd pretend to be much more able and independent then I really was—but everywhere I went, my wheelchair followed, contradicting my embellishments. It wasn't just the girls that I couldn't impress; concerned friends and parents of any girls that I dated seemed to always destroy the potential for a lasting relationship. To make matters worse, I couldn't drive. Homebound, I was sure I was destined to live the rest of my life watching.

My closest companion was the debilitating and ever-present nerve pain in my legs, which only added to my frustrations. Struggling with life, I waited for something to show me that I still had purpose.

I gazed longingly out the family room window at the mountains above our house.

My mom's voice interrupted my thoughts. "Can I do anything to help ease your pain?"

"This is the only freedom I have," I replied sullenly. "I get to daydream about living life while everyone around me is really doing it." I turned to her desperately. "This is not a life! I'm completely trapped!"

Sitting down next to me, my mom grabbed my hand. "Brandon, it could always be worse," she said lovingly. "You have a family who loves you and a nice home for you to find peace. If the Savior did not want you here, he would've taken you countless times already." She continued, "Since the day you were born, I knew that you were a powerful spirit and would be tested to the limits to make you become stronger. The Lord knows you can do this, and so do I."

I didn't reply, but I knew that she was right. All of my struggling *had* to be for a purpose beyond what I could understand. The hard part was trusting what I couldn't see.

Behind the scenes, my dad and religious leaders moved forward with their plans of taking me to the salmon capital of the world—a fisherman's paradise. Needing to get out of the house for a change of pace, I finally accepted the invitation to go. Determining to make the most of it, I told my dad, "I may not be able to catch a break in life, but I am going to catch a king salmon!"

King salmon not only are the largest and best tasting of the wild salmon, but they are also difficult to catch. The next two months would consist of me learning how. Frequenting every fishing shop in Utah, we searched for the right rod and reel for me to use for deep-sea fishing. The challenge was finding a rod and reel big enough for me to keep hold of. The only way for me to grab hold of anything is to lift my wrist, which automatically closes my fingers just enough to the palm of my hand to grip something. This technique is medically called a *tenodesis grasp*, and it allows me to grab on to big objects that don't require firm finger control.

My next challenge was figuring out how to not fall out of my wheelchair while battling the high seas and reeling in a fish. To remedy this task, I used my old weightlifting belt. Acting as a large seatbelt, it was used to strap my chest to the backrest of my chair, which gave me the support needed to stay upright.

During the day, I'd practice reeling in a ten-pound dumbbell off the blacktop of the church parking lot while wearing my weightlifting belt. As I carried my large fishing pole and reeled the weight in, I was sure people driving by must've thought that I wasn't just physically disabled but that I had lost my mind as well. It didn't matter to me; I was determined to catch my king salmon, and I practiced regularly until our departure date.

My dad and I, along with two of our church leaders and one of their sons, boarded the plane and headed to Ketchikan. As we approached the southwest corner of Alaska, snow-capped mountains came into view. Lakes snaked through them, feeding pristine rivers emptying into the Northwest Passage just below us. I felt like an eagle as I looked out the window while flying over this wilderness paradise. My dad, sitting next to me, pointed out the window and said, "Down there is your king salmon. Let's go catch it!" Excitement began to replace melancholy as my disability faded into the background and my old self emerged.

Once we landed, we took in our surroundings. The beauty around us was absolutely breathtaking. Bald eagles flew above us in abundance, calling to us to watch their majestic dominance of the sky. The air felt cleaner here and the greens looked brighter. If heaven is cold, it is Alaska.

Dropped off at a shuttle, we arrived shortly thereafter at the Cedars Lodge on the coast of Ketchikan, where we'd make our home for the next five days. Those days would be spent fishing together with our fishing guide. This trip was the first chance I'd had to enjoy the outdoors again with my dad, trolling the waters up and down the Northwest Passage amongst the bellowing humpback whales and occasional killer whale sightings. Pre-accident, fishing together was just one of the activities we did on a weekly basis. Fly-fishing at Utah's rivers and high mountain lakes was something my dad chose to never do again after I broke my neck. Going alone, he felt as if he were somehow cheating on me, so he stopped going altogether. Now, here we were, father and son, fishing just like old times. It felt incredible. The only problem was that at the end of each day, our boat remained void of our king salmon.

On our last day of the trip with only a couple of hours left on the boat, we headed back toward Cedars Lodge, again empty-handed. We had caught fish, but not the elusive king salmon I had so desperately wanted. The fishing guide was in the process of reeling our five fishing poles back into the boat as we rounded Prince Edward Island. A familiar feeling of being defeated while trying to accomplish something I could not needled its way inside me, bringing my disability back with it. Looking up at the beautiful blue sky above, I thanked God for the opportunity to come here, at the same time feeling brokenhearted that this once-in-a-lifetime chance would pass me by. Looking at my dad, I did my best to hide my disappointment before saying, "Thanks for bringing me here. Even without a king, it was still amazing."

The fishing guide, watching the interaction between my dad and me, spoke up. "Brandon," he said, "as long as my boat is in the water with you on board, we'll fish to the end." Stopping the boat, he smiled at me. "Let's put those lines back in."

Grateful for one last opportunity, I quickly agreed.

Once the lines were cast, the captain began to rigger down our fishing line to the appropriate sea depth for catching king salmon, now our only goal. A half hour quickly went by when suddenly out of the five fishing poles in the water, I saw mine begin to bounce violently. Looking back at the captain, my eyes went wide with excitement. Grabbing my pole while shouting in anticipation, the captain called to me, "Here's your king! It hammered your line!" Handing me my fishing pole, he shook his head, knowing how incredibly unlikely this was to happen in the last hour of our trip.

All excitement turned to sheer determination as my line speedily exited my reel, sending a buzzing sound through the air. Grabbing hold of my rod just like I had practiced for months, I knew this was my chance to accomplish something my morale needed. In desperation to keep hold of my rod, I embraced it to my chest, wrapping my arm and wrist around it. I grabbed the reel with my right hand, ready to bring in the king on the end of my line. However, all my practicing and best intentions were no match for this fight. Looking down, I watched the line escaping faster than I could reel it back.

"Brandon, you're losing line!" the captain shouted as my grip was quickly weakening.

"I can't hold on any longer! What do I do?!" I pleaded.

In that moment, I understood something that no one else on board that boat did. That question had a far deeper meaning for me. That question was not meant for the captain on our small fishing boat, and it wasn't about keeping the king on my line; I was pleading with my Captain and my King for help. I had lost my grip on life and any desire to continue. I was barely functioning. I didn't know how long I could hold on before ultimately losing my grip and letting it all go.

No longer aware of the chaos of people in the boat shouting at me and telling me what to do, I helplessly watched as the rod slipped further from my grasp. Once again, I was losing a battle that I could not win with my strength alone. I had to catch this fish. I had to know I had worth and that I could do something hard. I had to know that I could live this life I did not want.

Jolting back to my situation, I frantically began looking around the boat for something to help strengthen my weakness. Suddenly I saw hidden in a cubbyhole a brilliant idea. There sat a roll of duct tape. I shouted in excitement, "Dad, grab the duct tape!"

Without waiting for me to explain, my dad sprang into action, desperate to help me.

"You're going to duct tape my left hand to the fishing rod," I told him, "and my right hand to my fishing reel!"

Grabbing the duct tape, my dad immediately began binding my hands where I had instructed. Joking, but half serious, I looked at the captain and asked, "You're sure this is a king salmon on the end of the line, right?" I raised my eyebrows. "Because if I'm hooked on to a killer whale, I'm going to be bouncing like a flat rock across this ocean in about ten seconds." Everyone but me laughed. "I'm duct taped now, and there's no way I'm letting go!" I finished, determined.

The captain quickly eased my fears. Looking at me, he responded reassuringly, "This is your king, Brandon."

Something beautiful happened once my hand was bound to the rod: I had no fear of letting go, even while battling something that felt more like a ten-thousand-pound killer whale than a thirty-five-pound king salmon. With my new added security and strength, I began to get the upper hand, fighting while reeling in my line.

"You got this! Keep the rod up! Keep reeling it in!" my dad excitedly counseled.

I couldn't believe that out of all the fishing rods on the boat, this king chose to bite mine. As I continued fighting to reel in the king salmon, I felt like it had been placed specifically on my line by a loving Heavenly Father, so very aware of my struggles.

An hour went by of me exhausting every ounce of effort I could give, and then my moment finally arrived as my king salmon was pulled into the boat amidst cheers and hugs.

"That king chose your rod!" one of my church leaders exclaimed through tears.

My dad cut away the duct tape around my hands, and we embraced. The captain then laid the fish on my lap, and everybody cheered once more.

Using the fish and duct tape, God metaphorically taught me a basic truth that changed how I was battling my difficulties: To be effective in overcoming my challenges in this life, I have to put forth my *own* effort to the best of my ability in good days *and* bad. I need to choose to pray. I need to choose to read the scriptures. I need to choose to be happy, kind, loving, generous, humble, meek, and patient when I feel like being anything but. Those things are God's tools. They are the duct tape that binds us to Him, and they give us added strength to keep going when we have nothing left. I was also acutely aware that God never takes the duct tape away; He placed it there specifically for me. It was waiting, but it was always up to me to see it and use it.

Chapter 9

FINDING HIGHER GROUND

The church building across the street from my house was not just a place of spiritual refinement for me growing up; it also served as an outlet for my youthful energy. I spent countless hours in its gymnasium playing pick-up ball games with friends.

After I broke my neck, it was tough going over to the church gymnasium for the first time. Pushing only a few feet onto its hardwood floor, I suddenly stopped as emotion overcame me. Not-too-distant memories poured through my mind. I could hear the crowds cheering each time I scored, the buzzer signaling the quarter was over, and the laughter of family and friends as they visited together while watching the games. Finally, I remembered the many nights alone spent shooting basketballs through the hoop as I dreamed about cute girls, thought about life, and envisioned what my future had in store.

As the tears pushed their way out, I knew that my feet would never touch this hardwood floor again. But it wasn't just sadness that I felt in that moment—I cherished those memories on a whole new level. Even with a broken heart, I gazed at the gym, grateful for the opportunities it afforded me while growing up. As I pushed forward in my chair, I realized the gymnasium I had grown so fond of over the years wasn't done with me yet. This would now become the place where I would push myself physically in hopes of getting stronger. Only this time, crowds would not cheer me on, nor would the sounds of basketballs hitting the floor echo off the walls.

For years following my accident, that gymnasium and the parking lot would become well acquainted with me each time I was angry. There wasn't a square inch that didn't feel my four wheels constantly grinding over it as I emptied my emotions. This would become my safe space, a place where I could escape and water its dry surface with my tears. After months of pushing and not seeing results from these frequent workouts, I only pushed myself harder. Now, strapping Velcro weights around my arms and the frame of my wheelchair, I increased my hours spent there each day. My arms and shoulders screamed in pain while music blasted through earphones, drowning out their protests.

Absolutely exhausted one day after pushing around the church parking lot seven times, I saw an older neighborhood friend approach. After she greeted me, we talked briefly about my recovery thus far. I smiled before jokingly telling the older woman, "I'm here trying to get buff for my date later tonight."

Suddenly she stopped.

"It's going to be tough for you to get married," she said matter-of-factly, as if warning me that I was only going to get my heart broken if I pursued dating.

Dumbfounded at what had just occurred, I sat reeling at her comment, not even able to tell her that I did in fact have a date later that night. Stunned into silence, I started to question myself. *What does she mean by that? Am I not good enough? Because I'm paralyzed, it means my social life should be paralyzed too?*

To be honest, her remarks brought up my own deep-seated fear, which was just that. Getting married with my disability and all its baggage to the type of girl I wanted to marry would be a difficult uphill battle. The exchange only added to a growing depression I had to fight harder with each waking day. Taking off once again, I focused on pushing further than I ever had before.

Hours passed.

My soul was crying out, demanding my unmovable body to wake up! Eventually my Walkman ran out of battery power. As I went to take out my earplugs, I noticed blood dripping from each of my knuckles. Pushing so hard and for so long, I had rubbed my knuckles raw. Wiping the blood on my forehead as if it were war paint, I kept going, fighting for any semblance of independence and strength this broken body was willing to give to me.

It had been a year and a half since my accident. My only mental escape was in my daydreams, somewhere it seemed I was living more than in the present now. However, it soon became a toxic and constant reminder of not only what I had given up but also what I believed (and now obviously what others believed) I would never have in this life. I was so angry that I had lost my independence right at the prime of my life while everyone else was running with theirs.

Sitting at the computer one afternoon, I studied a recent family portrait. I hated the disability staring back at me with its counterfeit smile. Immediately, I moved through the workings of Photoshop, seeking to erase this blatant and cruel misrepresentation of who I was. The disability was literally robbing me of everything. Like a thief in the night, it slowly moved through my house, taking my most prized possessions and dreams. Gone were dating that actually led somewhere, work opportunities, outdoor activities I once enjoyed, hobbies, and even friends who in the beginning were there. I sat stripped bare and helpless with little left to offer. With the click of a single button, I deleted the image of this person who was not me, yet he was.

Erasing my picture was the precursor to seeing how life would look without me in it. It seemed that life would somehow be better if I were gone. Through all my years of dealing with depression, I had never once acted out on the dark thoughts that seemed to constantly be there. Deleting the picture and toying with the idea of removing me from life scared me.

My grip on life was weakening again.

That's when, on a sunny summer Thursday afternoon, an angel showed up at my door.

My mom answered the door. An aged and raspy voice asked, "Is Brandon home?"

My mom quickly replied, "Yes, he is. Come on in and I'll grab him for you."

This wasn't the response I was hoping my mom would give.

The man's voice didn't sound familiar, but I wasn't about to push over to the front door to find out who it was. I wanted to be left alone. Trying to think of any excuse not to see this person, I pushed back to my room to get away from him.

To my surprise, my mom brought the man into my bedroom. There was no place for me to hide, which my mom understood completely. I immediately recognized the elderly visitor as a neighbor who I'd see occasionally at church on Sundays.

The man could see that my eyes were red from crying, something that seemed to be happening constantly lately. Quickly, he reached out to me and patted me on the shoulder. "Brandon," he said, "I'm Press Jensen. Let's get you out of the house and go for a little joyride."

I looked at my mom with desperation in my eyes, as if to say, *Please, say something so I don't have to go.*

She smiled at me. "Press," she said, "I think that would be a great idea. Brandon would love to get out of here!"

She had boxed me in a corner that I could not roll out of. I hardly even knew this tall eighty-something-year-old man. Plastering on the phony smile I was becoming more and more accustomed to wearing, I reluctantly replied, "Sure, that sounds fun."

Once Press had gotten the keys from my mom, he insisted that I remain in my power chair for our secret excursion instead of my manual wheelchair that I normally used. I eyed my mom.

Unconcerned, she busied herself strapping me into the back of the van before sending us on our way. Before we left the driveway, Press Jensen looked back at me and said, "Don't tell your mom, but I'm taking you somewhere special to lift your spirits." He began to laugh. "If I told her where I'm taking you, she'd probably kill me."

Rolling my eyes internally, I thought, *Listen, Press. Bingo night down at the ole Lion's Club is not as crazy as it used to be.*

As we moved toward the freeway, Press asked, "So where would you like to go?"

"It doesn't matter to me," I responded, wondering why he was asking when he supposedly already had our date planned. "Wherever," I finished.

"Ahhh," Press Jensen said, thrilled that I had responded the way he had hoped. "Then it really doesn't matter *where* we go."

Did we literally just act out a scene from Alice in Wonderland *with the Cheshire cat?* I thought.

Driving past the state capital, we continued up the mountain bench overlooking the Salt Lake Valley. Curiosity now piqued, I asked, "So where *are* we going?"

"Brandon, I want to take you to a place that will broaden your vision," Press responded.

Not too much later, we pulled into the parking lot of Ensign Peak. With the help of my power chair, I exited the van.

With confidence, Press pointed up to the large mountain in front of us. "You see that peak?" he asked. "I'm going to help you climb it."

I looked up at the steep, rugged, rocky incline that made up the trail and thought, *He realizes I'm totally paralyzed, right? There's no way in the world my power chair can climb that.*

I was seriously nervous.

I'm going to die going up this mountain, I thought. *And if I don't die, then Press will, when he sustains a massive heart attack pushing me up it.* I had seen the oxygen that Press usually carted around with him. This was a respiratory disaster.

Grabbing the back of my power chair, Press confidently started pushing me up the steep mountain trail. "Just don't tell your mother about this," he said again.

I hate to tell you, I thought, *but she's going to find out when they find our bodies.*

What a sight we were for onlookers: an old man pushing a young man in a three-hundred-pound power chair up a steep mountain. After making it up the mountain as far as we could go, we stopped and looked out over the Salt Lake Valley. Mountains, tall buildings, trees, and the Great Salt Lake filled the landscape. It was beautiful. After momentarily taking in the sights, Press Jensen began to recount the story of those who first settled the Salt Lake Valley. He spoke of their difficult journey traveling over 1,300 miles by foot from Nauvoo, Illinois, before finally arriving here.

"Brandon," he said, "just like you, those pioneers had to push forward and fight every step of the way." He paused. "They were pushing handcarts. You're pushing your wheelchair."

I let his words sink in as he continued.

"Like you, they were tested to their limits physically, mentally, and spiritually. After their long journey, the first thing they did when they reached this valley was climb to the top of this very peak, on this very trail." He continued, "At that time, this overlooked a barren desert valley floor. And you know what?" he asked me. "They saw potential in that barren valley, like I see potential in you."

My soul in desperate need of being rescued, I began to feel inspired by his words and the view around me.

"Now look at this valley!" Press exclaimed. A large smile filled his face. "It's full of trees, homes, shops, and successful people. It took time, hard work, faith, vision, and patience, but look at what it's become. It's truly extraordinary."

He was right too. It *was.* I could not deny that. Without saying anything to each other, we gazed over the valley once more, taking it all in. I thought of many of the Old Testament prophets, like Abraham and Moses, and how they climbed to the peaks of mountains in hopes of being literally closer to the Lord while receiving His instruction. Not too long ago, Brigham Young had done the same thing when he had climbed to this very mountain peak in order to envision how to settle the valley. To be able to create their new home, he needed to stand high above the valley to see its entire potential. Once he was standing in higher places, he was able to survey the land and map out its future.[5]

---

5. "Lesson 36: 'The Desert Shall Rejoice, and Blossom as the Rose,'" *Doctrine and Covenants and Church History Class Member Study Guide* (1999).

It hit me—for the past couple of years I had sat in lower places by allowing myself to feel lost and depressed. From that low viewpoint, I could not see my potential. In stark contrast were the feelings now overcoming me. Once I could see the valley below with all its beauty, my horizon broadened, and so too did my perspective; what was happening to me now was momentary, but the lessons would be eternal and extraordinary.

Reaching into his jacket, Press pulled out a pair of binoculars and placed them around my neck. "Brandon, binoculars and life have one thing in common," he said. "Both require adjusting to changing conditions." He smiled down at me. "You've gone through a lot of changes already in your young life," he said. "Re-adjust your focus. Don't concentrate on what you've lost, but on what you still have." He looked down at me once more, eyes full of love. "You're still the same, Brandon," he said. "Focus on how Heavenly Father sees you. If you adjust your vision, your outcome will be as bright as your faith."

The lessons I learned that afternoon saved me, setting me back on the right mental path. Press Jensen and I became dear friends after that experience. That same set of binoculars still sits on the top of my dresser, serving as a daily reminder to me to re-adjust my focus on the positive in life whenever I feel down.

Returning home that day, I was determined to do better at being positive and choosing to stand in high places. I continued to push myself physically in the church parking lot as well as outpatient therapy alongside other paralyzed individuals. Desperately wanting to get stronger, I had done little else than work out for the past two years. Yet my muscles refused to strengthen like they had before my accident, since most of my nerve endings no longer fired. It was as if someone had cut the electricity to my muscles—regardless of how many times I flipped the switch, the lights refused to come on. With no flowing current, there was no way for my body to send the signals needed to build muscle and therefore no way for my muscles to respond. No matter how hard I worked and no matter how hard I pushed myself, nothing would or could physically change. The frustration of working harder than I ever had pre-accident with zero physical results was infuriating. The tried-and-true formula of hard work and exercise didn't apply to me anymore, and I refused to believe it. I was working harder than I'd ever seen any able-bodied person work out, and my physical payback was daily deterioration and atrophy. I could not stop the process.

Albert Einstein is often credited with saying, "The definition of insanity is doing the same thing over and over again but expecting different results."

One day while at outpatient therapy, the Spirit whispered to me to stop what I was doing and look around me. The gym was always filled with people like me, ranging from newly injured to thirty-plus years post-accident. Like clockwork, we'd show up each day. Many of us were paying our own way as years passed and insurance had long since stopped covering the cost. Every day we came with the same mindset: today would be different than yesterday. Today would be the day the lights would come back on.

All of us wanted the same thing and had allowed ourselves to become blinded by our demands. It made sense too. It's logical that some of our best feelings of independence came from the time we were all physically independent. Once that had been taken away, it was only natural to fight to get that freedom back. So focused on what we'd lost, we ignored what we could gain.

Seeing the gym's patrons in a whole new light, I suddenly saw mountains of untapped potential withering before my eyes. As I sat stunned by what I was realizing, I heard Press Jensen's voice in my mind: "Re-adjust your focus, Brandon. Don't concentrate on what you've lost, but on what you still have."

The Spirit then spoke to my soul. *Real independence isn't based on how strong your muscles are, but on how strong your faith in God is.*

Much of my focus pre-accident was on image, self-confidence, and physical strength. Now my Father in Heaven was trying to show me that there was an everlasting strength that mattered far more.

It's time to focus on what I want you to become, the Spirit would impress upon me. *What you and I always wanted you to become—a strong person.*

Images of me attending college and working and helping others through their own accidents came to my mind. I saw myself speaking in front of many people in various and diverse places. I saw that I was happy. Most importantly, I saw that my future self was spiritually stronger. While experiencing all of that, I also understood that so great was God's love for me that He would not force this outcome on me. He would allow me to continue to stay here and be who I currently was or to leave and choose to become something better.

Humbled, I rolled over to my physical therapists and thanked them for their help over the past two years before explaining that it was time for me to start a new chapter. "I will walk again, I have no doubt," I said. "Maybe in this life, but surely in the next!" With peace in my decision, I said a final goodbye before rolling out the front doors and leaving the gym in the past.

Chapter 10

THEY THAT BE WITH US

And when the servant of the man of God was risen early, and gone forth, behold, an host compassed the city both with horses and chariots. And his servant said to him, Alas, my master! how shall we do?

And he answered, Fear not: for they that be with us are more than they that be with them.

And Elisha prayed, and said, Lord, I pray you, open his eyes, that he may see. And the Lord opened the eyes of the young man; and he saw: and, behold, the mountain was full of horses and chariots of fire round about Elisha.

2 Kings 6:15–17

By now, I was becoming used to the ups and downs that being wheelchair bound often brought. Not only that, but I was very aware of the contrast between light and dark in my life. The adversary worked on me so strongly that at times I could physically feel the presence of his followers. In sharp contrast and more often, I could feel and at times hear and see God's angels. So strongly was I aware of God's power that I was able to dispel the darkness when needed and bring in God's light.

Though the thought of darkness surrounding us at times can be terrifying, the knowledge that light will always dismiss darkness should fill us with peace. Yes, darkness is there. Yes, I have had to and will continue to battle dark times. But even as the adversary lurks at my threshold seeking to lunge at me, I know that there are concourses of angels standing guard.

While I know of a surety that God can and does send heavenly angels, I also know that we have help from *both* sides of the veil.

Jeffrey R. Holland once said:

Not all angels are from the other side of the veil. Some of them we walk with and talk with—here, now, every day. Some of them reside in our own neighborhoods. . . . Indeed heaven never seems closer than when we see the love of God manifested in the kindness and devotion of people so good and so pure that *angelic* is the only word that comes to mind.[6]

Perhaps even more important than heavenly visitations are God's expectations of each of us. Many times, we are the very angels that God is trying to send to answer His children's prayers. I learned this principle from a man I only briefly met named Sam, whose encounter with me changed both our lives.

In my opinion, the biggest offense given to people who are different from us is neglect. Comparing my first eighteen years spent walking, fitting in socially, and even just being acknowledged

---

6. Jeffrey R. Holland, "The Ministry of Angels," *Ensign*, Nov. 2008.

to my last twenty years being in a wheelchair, standing out, and feeling neglected is a painful and sad experience.

Although I haven't changed internally, the perception of those who didn't know me in pre-accident social settings has. I notice people get fearful of saying the wrong things or looking at me the wrong way. So instead they glance away or say nothing. In those moments, they lose an opportunity that is easy and free. It costs nothing to make a positive impact in my life, or the life of someone else, simply by saying a friendly "hello."

When I am pushing my wheelchair in public places, I notice you not noticing me. When you make eye contact and talk to others in my group of friends but don't acknowledge me, I notice. When I look at you and your eyes quickly glance away from me as you walk by, I notice. The sharpest cut we can give to someone who is desperate to be acknowledged is to be silent.

The adversary uses negligence as a weapon to make those who feel ignored think they don't belong in society, don't have any real value in life, or can't make a difference. These feelings promote sadness about our lives and hate for ourselves and others in general. I know these feelings well.

One night I'd had enough of avoided glances and awkward stares. I vowed once again to my Heavenly Father in prayer that I would never act unkindly to those who may feel forgotten in our society. I promised I would never act in a manner that would make them forget who they truly are: children of God with divine potential. Finally, I vowed that I would help His children by answering His call of action whenever the need arose.

The great thing about prayer is that when you ask God to make you an instrument in showing charity to others, He tends to quickly provide you the opportunity.

While attending church services that following weekend, I saw an unfamiliar man sitting alone in the back of the church with his head down. To be honest, he looked a little intimidating and out of place amongst the other churchgoers. He had a hardened countenance that exposed a rough life. He wore a short-sleeved button-up shirt. I noticed the tattoos up and down both his arms. Seeing him in the back, I felt such compassion for him. His expression was one I recognized. I could relate to feeling alone amongst the crowd of *normal*.

The Holy Spirit spoke within me, letting me know this was my opportunity to be an instrument of God's love for someone else, as I had promised in prayer a week before.

Slowly, I pushed over to greet this visitor. Reaching out my hand, I said, "Hello, brother. It's so good to see you in church today! I wanted to let you know how grateful I am that you are here and how much the Lord loves you! My name is Brandon, and I know that by trusting in the Lord and following His teachings, He will help you overcome your challenges and give you everlasting peace and happiness."

Surprised those words had come out of my mouth, I eagerly anticipated his response.

I saw something beautiful happen.

Like watching the sun shine powerfully through the clouds after a storm, I saw his eyes quickly ignite, beaming with the light they had been missing only seconds before.

"It's a pleasure meeting you, Brandon," he said. "My name is Sam. I really appreciate those kind words."

The church organ started to play, signaling the meeting was about to begin. I told Sam that I'd love to catch up with him after church services before rolling back to where my parents were seated in the chapel.

After sacrament meeting was over, I looked in the back of the chapel for Sam. He was nowhere to be found. I never saw him again. As the years went by, however, I often wondered what became of him.

Six years later, he found me on Facebook and sent me a private message:

Hello Brandon, I doubt if you even remember me, but I briefly lived with my sister in Bountiful. We went to your church one day. My name is Sam. I have looked for you for years. I was really impressed with you. You were such an inspiration to me and I just wanted to thank you. In fact, you were such an inspiration to me that I named my first-born son after you.

I hope you are well. My regards to your family. Thank you so very much.

—Sam

To be honest, I didn't remember who Sam was, and here he had named his son after me. Realizing how much power and influence we each carry and how that can impact other's lives only strengthened my resolve to search out those in need of a friend. I quickly wrote Sam back, anxious to recall who he was.

Sam,

He must be a good-looking kid!

I'm truly honored by your kind words and am glad you found me on Facebook. I'm speechless that I left such a good impression on you, to have you name your son after me. I am inadequate for such an honor . . . but hope to live my life worthy of such esteem. I still continue to push forward.

My strength and inspiration continually comes from our Savior Jesus Christ, where I find great hope and faith through His teachings.

Hope you are well!
Please continue to stay in touch . . .

Sincerely,
Brandon

I'm so grateful he did stay in touch, because the rest of the story was truly incredible.

Brandon,

Hope you are well. I just wanted to explain why you mean so much to me and why I named my son after you. When I moved to Bountiful in 1999, I was really struggling. I was dealing with a lot of pain from my past because of my military experience and failed relationships. I was not on the right path. I went to Bountiful because I was running from my bad choices. Right before going to Bountiful, however, I went on a trip to Missouri.

I had never been there and didn't know where I was going or what was even there. I just felt compelled to go. I was absolutely broke, so I sold an old baseball card collection and went. I drove straight there and parked. I had prayed that once I got there, there would be someone there to help me. When I got out, I walked down a path. It was there that a man walked up to me. Without me asking, he explained some things to me that I needed to understand in that moment. When he left, he pointed to a spot and said, "Right there is the best place to pray. There you will find the answers to your questions." I did as he said. Not only did I receive answers, but I again prayed that there would be people in Bountiful to help me once I arrived. When I met you, I recognized you as a person I had seen in my mind during my prayer while in Missouri as someone that would help me.

I don't know who the man was, but another couple passed us while we were talking and didn't even acknowledge he was there.

When I arrived in Bountiful and went to church, you made me feel welcome. Something I was looking for. Something I always try to remember to do. While in Bountiful, I studied the scriptures and prayed. I set an appointment with the bishop to talk about my past in the Gulf War and my decision to deal with my PTSD by abusing alcohol, instead of prayer and repentance.

I still have trouble with the things I did and saw in my past. It still hurts but the burden of the survivor's guilt and alcoholism has been lifted. The joy of Heavenly Father's love has returned to my life. Thank you, I am so grateful for the kindness you showed me and for helping me when I needed it the most. Since then, I have been blessed with a wife, two beautiful sons and a wonderful life. I have received so many wonderful blessings I can't count them all.

I was planning to end my life, but you saved it. I would have never known the joys of life had you not.

—Sam

Sitting in stunned silence, I read Sam's message again. What I had done that day was nothing more than acknowledge someone who I hadn't seen in church before. The relationship between that minute choice and someone choosing to live overwhelmed me. It took me no more than a second to make that decision. It had required zero effort on my part and had not changed anything for me by doing it. Yet it had altered everything for a man I knew nothing about.

Humbled, I also realized that God knew He could send this man to me. He trusted me with one of His precious spirits. He knew that He would not have to explain to me why the man was covered in tattoos or the light was missing from his countenance. He knew He wouldn't have to plead with me to see past all of that and instead just see *His* child, someone in desperate need of help. He also knew that although I didn't have the tattoos, the hardened countenance, or the war experience or whatever else his struggle might be, our paths had intersected somewhere in the dark.

My heart was touched at what I had just been taught. In that moment, I understood why it is that God allows some of us to walk that dark and lonely path frequently: there are others there who do not know the way out. If you want to know how much God loves you, love others.

Just like I had the opportunity to do something miniscule to help Sam, there have been countless others who have answered my prayers, ministering to me in my many hours of need.

Tyler, one of my home health aides, is a perfect example of angels among us. I was a little apprehensive of him when he walked through my door with his six-foot-four burly frame and disheveled hair for the first time.

Not knowing what to expect, I joked, "I've never had a big brown bear help me before."

His eyes lit up, his face divulging an enormous smile. Then with humility matched by few others, he commented with enthusiasm about how grateful he was to have the opportunity to serve others, adding that he was looking forward to getting to know me and serving me.

He said it in such a loving way that I couldn't help but instantly love and respect him. As the days went on, he'd show up each morning right on time, happy to be there. As time passed, we got to know each other better.

Tyler had grown up in Northern California, where he'd endured a difficult childhood. His dad was physically and emotionally abusive to him. His siblings were favored, and they excelled in life while he struggled. Tyler would tell me stories of his dad often saying to him that he would never amount to anything, that he was too stupid to be successful in life. While

I was shocked at some of the stories Tyler recounted to me, not once did he ever speak badly about his father.

As Tyler grew older, he struggled with the scars of his past as negativity and self-doubt began to find passage within his soul.

Then one day Tyler picked up the scriptures and began to read. He discovered a Heavenly Father who loved *all* His children equally. Dropping to his knees, Tyler prayed and felt the love he so desired and that was missing from his mortal father.

Later he would read a passage of scripture that was equally impactful:

> So when they had dined, Jesus saith to Simon Peter, Simon, son of Jonas, lovest thou me more than these? He saith unto him, Yea, Lord; thou knowest that I love thee. He saith unto him, Feed my lambs.
>
> He saith to him again the second time, Simon, son of Jonas, lovest thou me? He saith unto him, Yea, Lord; thou knowest that I love thee. He saith unto him, Feed my sheep.
>
> He saith unto him the third time, Simon, son of Jonas, lovest thou me? Peter was grieved because he said unto him the third time, Lovest thou me? And he said unto him, Lord, thou knowest all things; thou knowest that I love thee. Jesus saith unto him, Feed my sheep. (John 21:15–17)

In California at the time, Tyler was successfully self-employed in the construction trade. He was always dropping off meals and giving money to the poor, as well as employing some of the local homeless. However, when the economy crashed in 2008, he lost his livelihood.

Moving to Utah, he tried to start over. That was when Tyler made the realization that it wasn't the money that made his life rich and meaningful; it was the use of his talents to provide loving service to others. So Tyler began working as a home healthcare aide.

I figured out Tyler was financially struggling. Only making around $12 an hour in this job, he was not earning enough money to live the life that he desired.

I asked him once why he didn't try to find a higher-paying job that would better provide for his needs. His response pierced me to the core: "I am afraid that I would lose myself. I feel the Savior wants me to serve others because that's what brings me the most satisfaction and happiness in life. Nothing else matters besides pleasing the Lord."

When I heard him say that, I broke into tears.

One day Tyler showed up unannounced to bring me a caramel cashew frozen custard. He knew from our time together that it was my favorite treat. At the time I was going through another rough patch, and he thought the treat would put a smile on my face. It surely did, but I knew that it was likely a sacrifice for him. This act of selfless love and service wasn't something that he reserved just for me either. He gave to countless others.

Tyler taught me a valuable lesson: one can never feel alone or forgotten when doing something positive for others. Tyler feels God's love for him more than any other man I know. He never felt forgotten or that he wasn't good enough under the love of his Heavenly Father.

This world is full of people like Sam and Tyler. Truly "they that be with us are more than they that be with them" (2 Kings 6:16). It doesn't take an angel to answer God's prayers—it just takes someone willing. Though we may not save someone's life, our love can surely touch it. From my experience, when we add value to people, God adds value to us.

Chapter 11

LEARNING TO DRIVE

During my long months of hospital recuperation in 1998, a doctor once told me that I would probably never drive again. If by some miracle I did get strong enough, he then added, I'd surely be limited to driving a van. For those who know me, I'm not a van type of guy.

I love trucks. Before my injury, I was driving a full-size F-250. As much as my doctor's statement hurt, I blocked it out of my consciousness and told myself that one day I would prove otherwise. I understood the perspective of the "doubters," but I was determined not to make their doubts my doubts.

Four long years later, my hardheaded determination achieved that very goal. Not only did I drive again, but I also wasn't limited to driving a van. The road to get there, however, was harder than I could have ever comprehended and would take me more than a year.

For most people, the difficult part of buying a car is purchasing the right make and model at the right price. For me, finding the right truck was easy. I spent a year thinking about the type of truck I wanted to drive before finally purchasing a beautiful candy-apple-red Ford F-150 quad-cab.

After my truck was retrofitted for me to drive, I quite literally had everything at my fingertips. A handlebar on one side of my steering wheel connected to the brake and gas. Pushing the handlebar forward with the palm of my hand would cause the vehicle to brake, and pushing the bar down gave it gas. A steering device with hypersensitive power steering allowed me to turn the steering wheel. Three equally spaced pegs, attached to the steering wheel, helped me rotate it 360 degrees.

After I purchased my truck, it sat in my parents' garage untouched for months. I'd frequently go outside to give it some neglected attention and stare up at it longingly. It didn't help that I often dreamed at night of driving my truck while envisioning the freedoms of the open road. Opening the driver's-side door, I'd look up at the steering wheel and think, *You're going to give me my freedom back.* This goal of driving a truck was like trying to tame a wild mustang. I was determined to break it and ride. I had to. My soul and body were simultaneously screaming for independence.

My body literally feels bound, like I'm being wrapped up in a cocoon that I'll never break free from. So overwhelming are the feelings of being trapped that they often make me anxious. Anxiety then turns into frustration, which inevitably turns into depression and then anger. My body has so much pent-up energy, and it screams to be used all the time. I had to find some form of movement that could at least give me a sense of breaking free. I was determined to find a way to get into and drive my truck unassisted.

With immobile fingers, legs, stomach muscles, and triceps, I knew full well that my desire and goal would be nearly insurmountable, mainly because to drive a car, one needs to be able to get into a car.

Desperately and for weeks I combed the internet to find any type of solution that would enable me to transfer into my truck. I needed to be able to hoist myself into the truck, slide from my wheelchair into the driver's seat, store the wheelchair in the pick-up bed, and buckle my seat belt—all on my own.

After endless hours of research, I found a company that made an extendable driver's seat for the disabled. These geniuses created a driver's-side lift system—the key to getting me in and out of the truck. They also offered a small crane that mounted to the bed of the truck, designed to pick up and lift a wheelchair into the back. Excitement coursed through me as I began to see my fantasy slowly work its way to reality.

For hours upon hours I practiced in my parents' garage, trying anything to get myself into the truck. However, without the ability to use my triceps, it was nearly impossible for me to lift my backside off my wheelchair cushion, let alone up and over my wheelchair wheels, which were elevated two additional inches. Every time I tried to push upward, I flopped forward like a rag doll. I tried for months.

My parents would cautiously watch me as I precariously tried to transfer. Many times, my arms would give out. Without any use of my stomach muscles, I'd lose my balance and fall to the ground. My parents literally caught me several times right before my head smacked into the concrete garage floor. After more than a few times of this, my parents were not optimistic and often voiced their concerns. How could I blame them? They were already caring for a paralyzed son who had previously suffered a major head trauma. The last thing they wanted was to care for a son with additional brain damage on top of an already difficult disability.

But I could not let this go. "I understand your concern," I told my parents one day. "I'm worried too, but I believe with more time, I'll be able to figure this out."

My mom still looked nervous. "I hope so," she said. "Because if not, this will be one very expensive mistake."

She was right too. With the costly conversion, I was already thousands of dollars into the truck. If this didn't work, then I had wasted my life savings, as well as other generous donations from family and friends within my community.

Despite their fears, my mom and dad also understood how life changing driving would be for me. We all prayed daily that somehow I could figure this out. My sanity, and likely theirs, depended on it.

One evening I was by myself in the garage. Snow was falling outside. I watched it just start to blanket the driveway as a memory began to work its way into the corner of my mind.

During my senior year of high school, there was a massive snowstorm on a Thursday night. Cameron and I thought that school would surely be canceled on Friday, so we planned to go snowmobiling the next day up in the mountains. To our amazement and bewilderment, it was announced on the news the next morning that school for Bountiful High would still be in session. We reasoned that if we had to go to school, then we might as well go on snowmobiles. This is called logic when you are an eighteen-year-old boy.

Gassing up the sleds, off we went, taking a few detours on our way. We started the day off right with a gas station breakfast. Parking our sleds in a couple of parking stalls, we walked in with our snow gear and helmets on and ordered some food. After we'd had our fill, we got on our steel horses and ran. Understand that this was not normal within city limits and the foothills of Bountiful. Not only was it not normal; it wasn't legal.

It's amazing how emboldened and invisible you feel when you're dressed head to toe in snow gear, your head completely concealed inside a helmet. It's the whole "baby playing peek-a-boo" thing: if I cover my eyes, then you disappear. Going up and down the main road, we rode like we owned the streets, flying past cars driving in the opposite direction. Many of the drivers honked at us while shaking their heads in disbelief. Off we went with our testosterone, pride, and teenage arrogance to school.

We were fashionably late, with school already in session as we drove through the student parking lot. It was quiet as the snow continued to fall. As we pulled into the parking lot, we gassed and revved our engines, interrupting an otherwise peaceful start to Friday-morning classes. Looking up, we were pleased to see every window plastered with faces peering out, wondering who we were. Lighting our fuses and igniting our pride, we decided to put on a show for our fans.

Up and down the student parking lot we drove like we were on a drag strip before wildly making circles around the seminary building. Here we again stopped the flow of education (albeit a higher level of learning) right in its tracks. By then we had virtually shut down all secular and spiritual learning at Bountiful High School. Kids were either cheering us on or rolling their eyes. We didn't mind either reaction since they didn't have a clue who we were.

Besides, our defiant protest at not receiving our earned snow day wasn't just on our behalf—it was for all students who had gotten hosed that day, not just in Bountiful. This was for any student who had ever been robbed of a snow day throughout the history of the world.

With all the attention we were receiving, we knew there was no way we could go to school. We also knew that our time of basking in the limelight would be short. The curtain would soon close. Suddenly we both became paranoid, figuring the cops had to be on their way.

After one last victory ride around the school, we brilliantly pulled back inside the student parking lot, taking one last look at all the smiling faces. Not seeing any reason to listen to instinct at that point, we made a conscious decision to get off our snowmobiles and raise our arms in defiance, while yelling and laughing at the spectacle we'd caused.

Blaring red lights flashed as they made their way through the parking lot. Instinctively, Cameron and I both knew what we had to do. After the glory of our spectacle, there was no way we were going to let the man shut us down in front of our peers. Quickly jumping onto our snowmobiles, we took off at full throttle.

The miniscule amount of reason one is given at that age started processing. I was in a high-speed chase with several cop cars. Flying through an intersection, we proceeded to go up the street at eighty miles an hour. Cameron was a hundred feet in front of me. We pulled into Cameron's yard and ran to Barton Creek to hide. After what seemed like a lifetime, we walked out on foot to the road, only to be greeted by four cops with billy clubs drawn. This may not seem unusual if you live in a crime-ridden city, but for those of us who live in Bountiful and sleep with our doors unlocked, this is about as hardened a criminal as one can get. We were lucky not to get strip searched and thrown into the slammer.

With their bullhorns they shouted, "Freeze! Hands above your head!"

We knew we were dead.

In our foolishness, it didn't dawn on us that the officers could easily track us by the trail we had left from our snowmobiles. To our amazement, they had us surrounded. We were immediately verbally chastised before taken into custody. We both were sentenced to extensive community service after that one. On a more positive note, this experience showed me how many different and marvelous ways one can serve throughout his or her community.

In moments of sheer helplessness, these memories of lost independence that are not too far distant, yet a lifetime away, wreak havoc on my mind.

Sitting there in my wheelchair, I reluctantly decided to spend more time working on what would have been a breeze for the boy on the snowmobile but seemed impossible for this quadriplegic body. As I opened my truck door, sadness melted into anger. Frustrated and desperate, I lowered the driver's-side seat down again.

I would try one last time before calling it a complete failure. Again, I went through the motions of trying to get myself into the cab. Again, I tried to transfer into the driver's seat, and again, I could not lift my lower body off my wheelchair. Memories began to pour through my mind of things I could once do so easily. My heart broke. Out of helplessness and sheer desperation, I began to cry. Rolling my chair over, I bowed my head and placed it on the open driver's seat door.

"Heavenly Father," I began. A tear rolled down my cheek as I earnestly started to pray. "Please help me figure this out." I paused, not sure if I wanted to know the answer to what I was about to ask. "Is this even possible? What should I do?" I asked helplessly before closing my simple prayer.

I sat for a few minutes with my forehead firmly planted on the door, tears now flowing down my cheeks. Abruptly, my wheelchair started to roll backward, stemming from the pressure of my head leaning against the open door. My brakes weren't holding. *Oh no! I'm going to fall out of my chair!* I thought. My legs and bottom started rolling away from where my head still lay resting on the door. I knew that at any second, the rest of my body would follow. Expecting to fall out of my chair, I braced for impact and got a miracle instead.

My chair stopped rolling away, but my head remained firmly planted against the door. I had found my balance point! Quickly, I reached back with my hand to lock down on my wheelchair brakes. With my chair now secure and my head still firmly planted on the truck doorframe, I held my breath. I then tried to lift my lower body up, now without the worry of losing my balance as my head held my body fast in place. Slowly my body lifted up and then over the wheels, the very thing I had tried to accomplish for months. I then successfully transferred over to my driver's seat.

I had done the impossible.

This time tears of joy ran down my face as I began to scream, "I did it! I did it! I did it!" Laughing out of sheer relief, I was immediately taken back to the desperate prayer I had only moments ago voiced. Humbled, I knew this wasn't happenstance or luck. Not only was this prayer answered, but also countless others voiced by me, as well as others in my behalf. My wheelchair had been directed exactly where it needed to end up for my success. I had to get to a state of complete and sheer exhaustion, forcing me to bow my head forward and place it where it needed to go, for the Lord to answer *my* prayer.

Immediately, I grabbed the lanyard wrapped around my neck and called to my parents through my cell phone. "You'll never believe what just happened!" I said. "Guess what chair I'm sitting in!"

Moments later, the door that led from the house to the garage was flung open. My parents rushed into the garage before stopping dead in their tracks. Relieved and thrilled, they jumped in the car while I took them on a joyride around the very streets where I had ridden my snowmobile four years previously.

Now, when I find myself struggling physically, mentally, and spiritually, I reflect on where my head is going. Does my head go toward anger, fear, sadness, or bad choices? Or does it go toward Christ, faith, hope, strength, happiness, and good works? Just like my ability to transfer my body successfully depended on where my head went, so too does it in life. Wherever your head goes, your body will follow.

It would take me many more months, after that day, to independently get in and out of my truck and drive. Yet enthusiasm drove me forward, and every moment of learning to drive again was pure joy.

Chapter 12

COMMUNITY COLLEGE

Someone once said that observing me get out of my truck is like watching a death-defying circus act. Honestly, that's a pretty good comparison.

I had just arrived at the University of Utah. It was a beautiful spring morning. The sun was shining, highlighting thousands of tiny buds on the trees that lined the streets. Tulips radiating every color of the rainbow were planted in precise lines on the grounds. This was my last semester in the social work program before I would earn my master's degree, an achievement that had seemed physically and mentally impossible when I first undertook it years before. Now here I was, almost finished. A large reason this was even possible was thanks to my truck and my ability to drive to and from school. I loved driving my truck daily. When I was driving, no one knew I was paralyzed. I was just a guy in a car like everyone else. The feeling of regained independence was incredible.

Pulling into the parking lot, I put the car in park and began the process of exiting my truck. Opening my driver's side door, I grabbed my handheld controller that extends my seat and me outside the door. Most of the time this works great, but it's still something I must be very cautious about. There are all kinds of things that can go wrong. I use my thumb and chin to push buttons on controls that are used to get me to and from the ground—a task that took me years of dedicated practice to master. If a button is pressed for too long, my wheelchair dangling from a rope and attached to a crane can potentially turn into a giant wrecking ball. It could smash into not only my truck but also the car I'm parked next to.

That day everything was going according to plan. My seat was now outside the truck. Five feet above the pavement with my legs dangling feels to me like I'm sitting on the edge of a high rise, but without any stomach muscles to keep me from falling over. There is always a bit of fear in me each time I take the risk to transfer.

That day I gambled and almost lost. As misfortune would have it, right as I sat perched above the ground, a leg spasm hit, sending me sliding forward on the chair. I flung my right arm like a grappling hook up and over my shoulder. It lay there haphazardly hooked onto my backrest, the only thing keeping me from doing a Humpty Dumpty.

"Somebody, if you can hear me, I need help! I'm falling!" I shouted for a miracle, hoping that somebody would respond. My panic-filled eyes scanned the empty student parking lot. It was filled with cars, but no one was in sight.

Knowing that if I fell it was going to be a long and costly process to put me back together again, I quickly grabbed my crane controller that picks up my wheelchair. With the thumb on my left hand, I pressed the buttons that sit the wheelchair down on the ground. Even as the wheelchair was moving, I could feel my arm start to lose its hold on my backrest.

This time, as I began to slip further, I didn't yell out loud but instead fervently prayed. "Dear Father in Heaven, I'm grateful for the opportunity I have to attend school this morning," I said. "Please send somebody down my parking stall to catch me. In the name of Jesus Christ, amen."

There have been countless times in my life, as I am sure there have been in yours, when somebody has come out of the blue to catch me figuratively—and literally—before I fall. Looking back on these experiences, it's as if the Lord placed someone there for me in those instances of greatest need. I don't doubt that He did and He does. This was one of those times.

It wasn't ten seconds later that a student came running over.

"Hey," he said, "I thought I heard somebody yell. Do you need some help?"

Relief washed over me.

"You are the answer to my prayers," I told him. "Please hurry and help me before I fall."

Quickly grabbing my legs, which were sliding off the chair, he helped safely lower my driver's seat down to where my feet could touch the pavement. He then helped me transfer to my wheelchair.

My simple prayer, combined with someone else's act of faith by following an impression, was the difference between a long recovery and successfully graduating from college two months later.

As I rolled to class that day, I thanked God, understanding full well that the outcome could have been far different for me. Almost falling out of my truck was only one of about a million difficulties I encountered while attending school. I marveled at the incredible journey it had been as I began to think back over the past eight years and all that had gotten me here.

College wasn't the natural choice for me. The easier decision would have been to sit at home and survive this disability. I was finally getting used to my daily routine and felt safe and secure at home. However, I didn't want to just survive my circumstances; I wanted and needed to live. Since I couldn't move physically, I needed to find movement spiritually and mentally. My next logical step was getting a higher education. As a bonus, I could now drive myself to school. I had to be present in society, no matter how difficult that would be. I was alive, after all. Staying home served me nothing. I knew life's on-ramp would be steep and challenging for me, but I was understanding more and more that life is all about moving forward. Having made the determination to go to school, I found myself seated in the counselor's office at the University of Utah.

"Brandon, show me your high school transcripts and your ACT score," the student counselor said to me.

My face instantly fell.

"You've taken your ACT . . . right?" she asked.

"No, I never took the test," I responded with worry. "That's not going to be a problem, is it?"

Looking at her face, I knew the answer to my own question.

Immediately, panic and dread began to flow through me at the prospect of not being able to go to school. Though this feeling was familiar to me after my brain injury, I expected to never feel it again once I graduated from high school—mostly because I didn't anticipate going to college. Now here I was back at school, older but feeling like a small child stuck in the counselor's office, once again not having a clue how this was all going to work out.

The counselor looked at me sympathetically.

"To get into this college and others in Utah, you need to score well on your ACT."

My heart began to race at the thought of taking the test. Suddenly I was back in eighth grade, post–traumatic brain injury, seated on the front row in Ms. Johnson's English class.

A tough, strict, and seasoned schoolteacher, Ms. Johnson demanded attention and respect in her class. It's hard keeping teenagers focused and quiet for any length of time. I'm sure having taught school for thirty-plus years hardened her teaching practices, causing her to be burned out on youth's immaturities. No student dared to get on her bad side. Fear of her unleashing fire and brimstone upon the entire class as a result was prevalent amongst all her students. If one student got on her nerves, like a teetering stack of dominoes, we'd each eventually get touched by her wrath. No one was immune, including me.

As hard as I tried, my TBI made it impossible for me to keep up with my homework, and my grades suffered tremendously as a result. It was not for a lack of effort or desire on my part—I spent many hours above and beyond what my peers spent on their homework. Regardless, my assignments and test results showed little signs of my hard work. I was in total survivor mode, just trying to hang on and keep up with my peers. I dreaded when teachers asked that our spelling tests be passed to another classmate to be corrected. I knew that whoever corrected my paper would think I was a dummy. I didn't want to bring any more attention to my shortcomings, but that's exactly what happened one afternoon.

It started just like any other day in Ms. Johnson's class. We had been discussing several chapters of our assigned reading from *The Diary of Anne Frank*. Our assignment was to write a brief sentence on the board about our thoughts and feelings on a chapter. For these types of scenarios, I would bring a device called a Franklin Speller. It looked like a calculator, but instead of numbers, there were letters on the individual keys. My parents had bought it for me to help me spell. My teachers knew never to call on me first, so that I would have time to look up various words and their correct spellings. Whether Ms. Johnson forgot or didn't fully understand my situation, she called my name.

Awkward silence followed for about ten seconds. *Why is she doing this to me? She knows better than to call on me first*, I thought. Dread fell over me. I knew that my classmates would not only see but also correct my horrible spelling as I wrote my sentences. *Doesn't everyone in the world, or at least the entire junior high, know about my brain injury? How has she forgotten?* I questioned. Remaining firmly planted in my seat and panicked, I didn't know what to say.

"Hurry, Brandon, chop chop! Let's go!" Ms. Johnson's voice filled the room.

"No. You go ahead and ask som-som-somebody else," I replied with my stutter, knowing full well that I had just committed treason.

The entire class stared at me, dumbfounded. I had refused her request. Everyone knew fury was about to be unleashed and we would all pay dearly for my stupidity.

This time she didn't ask but yelled, "No, Brandon, I asked you! Come up now!"

I was in no-man's territory. No boy or girl in my class wanted to be in my shoes. I tried to calm her anger by smiling and jokingly responding, "No, thank you. Please ask somebody else. I'm not going to write my sentence on your board right now."

Any person who has ever known a firm teacher may have experienced that joking with them when they are already at an eight does not, in fact, calm their anger but instead may immediately escalate it to a twenty.

The environment in the room went thermonuclear! Ms. Johnson threw her book down on her desk while yelling, "GET OUT OF MY CLASS!" With her laser focus staring right into my eyes, she pointed her finger at the classroom door.

The classroom was shell-shocked. I had challenged power and authority. In disbelief, I walked out of class, knowing that this situation should've never happened. Shaking, I made my way to my counselor's office and told her that I needed to call my mom.

Over the phone, I recounted everything that had happened. My mom's voice went from concerned parent to angry mother faster than a racecar goes from zero to sixty. From her tone, I knew I had just unleashed "mother bear." Surely this had to be the all-powerful antidote to Ms. Johnson.

I heard my mom's even voice. "Go back to class," she instructed. "I'm coming."

My mom can be very intimidating and direct with others when needed. Add overwhelming confidence and her piercing mastery of direct communication, and it's a deadly recipe, one that would make anyone standing in her way tuck into the fetal position.

It was a long walk back to Ms. Johnson's class. I wasn't so much concerned for myself at that moment as I was for

Ms. Johnson. As my mother's son, I knew this rare yet effective wrath intimately. I would not want to be in my teacher's shoes in the next ten minutes. My classmates and teacher were in for one heck of a show.

Opening the door to my class, I quietly took a seat near the back without any flak. I found it hard to concentrate, though, so I stared at the countdown clock, waiting for the fireworks to commence.

And then there it was.

The door to the classroom flew open.

"Ms. Johnson!" I heard my mom yell. "We have a problem, and we need to talk now!"

My startled teacher responded, "No. I'm in the middle of a class."

I sunk into my chair, my fingers gripping the sides tightly. Ms. Johnson obviously did not understand that my mom did not appreciate the word "no." My mom had just challenged the most feared teacher in all of junior high, probably across America, and Ms. Johnson had attempted to deny her. Lion had just met tiger, and this would be met with immediate, devastating, and resolute consequences.

As my mom entered the room, I slumped deeper in my seat. It was like watching the Discovery Channel. The lion was no longer stalking the prey—she was about to pounce. Walking closer to Ms. Johnson, my mom responded, "Don't you tell me to walk away. I'll gladly talk about it in front of your class if you'd like!"

Ms. Johnson could see that she had met her match. Quickly rushing my mom out of the classroom, she shut the door behind them. All my peers were staring at each other with "what just happened?" looks on their faces. A few students asked who that was.

With a smile, I responded, "That's my mom."

Ironically, the very thing I had feared the most as a kid had just become my mom's greatest quality as far as I was concerned. Fifteen minutes passed before Ms. Johnson finally returned. I would've given anything to be a fly on the wall during that heated conversation.

The bell rang shortly after, and Ms. Johnson came up to me and said how sorry she was. Word soon got around to the other teachers of The Incident. I was treated very well by all my teachers throughout my junior high years after that.

The memory of Ms. Johnson's class brought with it not only sentiments of the impossible but also a clear knowledge of just how hard I had to work to get through school back then. Now here I was needing to do it all over again, only this time with a new disability and new challenges and insecurities.

I sighed and looked up at the counselor.

"I'm sorry, your name again?" I asked her.

"Miss Davis," she quickly replied.

I looked her in the eye. "Miss Davis, I don't know what to do. If I were to give you my high school transcripts, the only A you'd see is from gym class." I smiled at her. "If I were to get graded on gym today, I'd fail miserably!" I joked. "Regrettably, the rest of my grades are all Cs and Ds. After my head injury, which I know you know nothing about, learning became terribly difficult. As hard as I tried, those are the grades I always received." I paused. "Four years ago, I was planning on working in the construction field, pounding nails and installing plumbing. How many people in wheelchairs do you know that are framing roofs?" I asked her, still trying to joke good-naturedly while emotion neared the surface. I paused again. "What I'm trying to say, Miss Davis . . ." I could feel the tears coming to my eyes, betraying my true emotions. "After how hard I worked just to graduate from high school, I never thought I would go to college." Swallowing hard, I finished, "I never thought I would be in a wheelchair either . . . yet here I am doing both."

I could see the counselor growing sympathetic to my situation.

"I know this is going to be a challenge for me," I said, "but I also know that I can be a better student than I was in high school." I smiled at her. "I've been through a lot. I just need a chance."

"Brandon, I believe you," Miss Davis replied, clearly moved. "Let me help you. I think I know where you can start your education." She paused. "Now, it's not a college you have in mind. It's a community college. You'll have to retake a lot of your high school English and math courses too, but if you score well and get your associate's degree, then I believe that you can get accepted to this college, or any other major college in Utah."

Thanking her, I rolled away determined to get back to the University of Utah one day—and to get As. Later that week, I enrolled in Salt Lake Community College, and the next phase of my journey began. The one thing I did not expect was that I would be getting and giving an education I had not registered for.

Chapter 13

EDUCATED

The night before my first day of classes, I hardly slept as I anticipated going back to school. Though I did not know what to expect, I was excited.

That morning, by the time I transferred into my truck, I felt like I was both ready for the day and exhausted enough to go back to sleep. Getting out the door and to school each morning would take me four hours with the help of an aide. It was physically draining. Still, as I drove down the road, I felt like I was finally merging back into society, and I loved it.

Looking around at the other people driving their cars, I finally felt normal again. Here I blended in. In my car, I could keep up with everyone else without standing out. For a short time, I am free from the bondage of my chair, and I revel in it. Turning the music up and letting my V8 engine take over, I jammed to "Life Is a Highway" by Rascal Flatts, feeling for a moment like my old self.

As I pulled into an empty disabled parking spot in the Salt Lake Community College parking lot, a mischievous smile escaped my lips. I remembered doing this very thing years ago in high school, though at that time I was neither disabled nor paralyzed. I was, however, always running late. Often I'd have to park in the back of the student parking lot and run as fast as I could to make it to class on time. Huffing and puffing, I'd usually enter class two minutes after the bell had already rung, resulting in a big fat tardy on my attendance record.

To remedy this situation, I decided to start parking in the disabled parking stalls. I didn't know of any disabled people that attended our high school, and the spots were begging for some attention. Even better, they were the closest parking stalls to school. Technically I could show up late and still make it to class on time. Unfortunately, the high school police officer recognized such a blatant parking violation and stuck a twenty-five-dollar ticket to my windshield. Knowing I wouldn't have to pay for the ticket until the end of the school year, I decided to make the most of his gift. As if I'd found Willy Wonka's Golden Ticket, I entered the wondrous land of disability parking at Bountiful High School. That ticket camouflaged my truck, enabling me to park in any parking stall, legit or made up, at school for the next four months. I guess the officer just assumed somebody must've beaten him to the punch when he'd see it on my windshield each day.

They aren't kidding when they say karma eventually comes back to bite you.

Parking in a disability stall at the community college that day still felt like I was breaking the law, even though I now legitimately qualified for such VIP parking "privileges."

Carefully transferring myself from my driver's seat to my chair, I smiled to myself. *I can't believe I'm doing this on my own,* I thought. The many months practicing in my garage paid off. I was ready for the challenge. When I had lain newly paralyzed in a hospital bed, I didn't know if I would ever get out of it.

Now here I was four years later, still paralyzed, but independent. It was an amazing feeling.

Late once again, I began pushing across the campus. It wasn't long before I was exhausted. With shoulders now burning, I looked up at the building that housed my class and saw something that made me shake my head in disgust. A long, steep "wheelchair-accessible" ramp led to the front doors. With a backpack filled with school books attached to the back of my chair and weighing me down, there was no way I would be able to wheel myself up the ramp. Looking at my watch and the entrance to the door thirty yards away, I saw people walking quickly back and forth, up and down the stairs, all of them oblivious to my predicament.

I didn't notice faces. Instead, my attention was glued to their legs. I watched them easily go up and down the stairs. It was nothing out of the ordinary for them, so simple it was mindless. I looked down at my legs as if to say, "See! This is what you're supposed to be doing for me! You're not any help! You are useless appendages that I have to cart everywhere!" As I watched my lost freedom blatantly parading in front of me, the frustration built inside of me. It was so hard for me just to get here. Now there were mountains in the shape of slopes and inclines. Not even *I* could climb the ramps put there for me.

All of this just so I could attend a single class—and I had more than one, all in different buildings. I suddenly and painfully realized what going back to school would truly entail. I wanted to scream! Continuing to watch the sea of legs enviously, I felt the frustration grow inside me. It wasn't long before my mind rescued me, taking me far away.

I, along with my family, had been invited by the football coach of BYU to attend Thursday's football practice. Each week a local hero was chosen and invited to join the team. This week that privilege had been given to me.

From the sidelines I watched the football players as they did their pre-season training. Sweat dripped from their brows. Once-pristine uniforms were now stained with dirt and grass. The players looked wasted and beat, probably wondering if they had anything left to give. Some even looked like they might vomit or pass out. Surely they longed for this practice to be over. All they wanted to do was sit down. All I wanted to do was stand up. Their "hell week" was my heaven.

I heard someone calling my name. Looking up, I watched as the coach motioned for me to join him on the field. I hadn't planned on this and didn't know what he wanted me to do or say. What I did know was that I was not going to have anyone help push me out onto that field. Though I knew it would be very difficult for me to push myself on the uneven grass, somehow I knew that these players needed to watch me do it, especially after what they had just done. I wanted them to put their fleeting and momentary struggle in perspective as they watched me move slowly toward them.

When I finally got to the center of the field, the team was gathered in a huddle. The coach looked at me. "Brandon, we are honored to have you here with us. Would you like to say anything?"

Unprepared, I was now seated in front of seventy guys roughly my age, all stronger and faster than me, all waiting to hear what I had to say. Funny how something that was once one of my greatest weaknesses and would have mortified me as a youth became the very thing I loved to do. It's amazing how quickly life rotates us between strong and weak.

Studying these athletes momentarily, I noted their strong backs, legs, arms, and abs. Each was the pinnacle of physical health, with muscles that grew and moved as they did. More than that, I saw my old self clearly. I knew what they saw when they looked in the mirror. I also knew that they loved, as I once did, what looked back at them. I remembered the feelings well. I was acutely aware that they had no idea what it would mean to lose all of it. I then knew what I needed to say.

"Brothers," I began, "I want you to understand a valuable lesson: if you put all your purpose and value into what you can physically do on the field, sooner or later in life, you're going to be disappointed," I said. "Your lives have to mean more than what you can do on this field, because these days will pass quickly." I looked them individually in the eyes, as if willing them to somehow understand what I was telling them without the personal knowledge of my words. I continued, "Build your foundations of self-worth in things that will last the test of time: your faith and relationship with God, your relationships with family and friends, helping and serving those in need, and anything else that will make you spiritually stronger." I paused. "These anchors of strength can't be taken away when our physical capabilities change from trials like mine or from something as simple as old age. In fact, they will grow stronger regardless of physical health, trials, and age." I said, "Some of the happiest people I know find purpose not in what they can achieve physically but through actions, words, and deeds. Place your worth on those things."

As I finished, the coach asked me if I would like to close with a prayer. There was a powerful spirit that accompanied that prayer. I thanked our Heavenly Father for the opportunities we have to prove ourselves on the field of life so that we may rise victorious over our adversaries, before asking that He help us overcome weaknesses through Christ and return to live in His glory. Truly that day we were taught as brothers that life is about so much more than a fleeting game played on a field.

After I was done speaking, the coach presented me with a signed helmet, football, and a "Y" flag. He then showed me his team's flag that they carry out of the tunnel each game. This flag was filled with signatures of people they deem as their heroes and examples. Asking me to sign my name amongst the others, the coach addressed the team, "Let this serve as a reminder to all of us to be a leader and a role model both on and off the field."

As the memory of those words faded in my mind, so too did my anger.

Looking at the ramp in front of me again, I said a quiet and brief prayer, asking for patience and help. After a moment, the Spirit then whispered to my soul, telling me that my purpose here wasn't just about receiving an education but also about giving one.

It became clear to me what I needed to do. I had to allow others to help me, which in turn would help them. I had to swallow my pride and be willing to provide myself as a constant service opportunity.

I stopped the very next person that walked by. "Excuse me," I said. "Could you help me get up this ramp?"

After that moment, everywhere I went throughout college, someone was always by my side. I never pushed alone. In fact, I hardly ever pushed at all. Someone was always willing to do it for me. It wasn't that people were oblivious because they wanted to be; they simply didn't know I couldn't do it on my own. Once they understood, they were always happy to help. And aren't we just like that as human beings? Once we understand the big picture, once we see another's wheelchair, do we not then notice the gift of our own legs? The burdens others carry are oftentimes the gifts we have been blessed with. I believe that is not by coincidence but by divine design. We are here to push and be pushed by each other.

Once I saw the power in giving and receiving daily service while going to and from classes, even if I could do it on my own, I usually chose instead to ask someone else, knowing we would both be blessed in the process. It became very rewarding for me before each class to decide who would be my Sherpa. Sometimes I'd pick a cute girl just so I could talk to her, but mostly it wasn't about me. I let the Spirit decide whom it was that I should ask for help. Not surprisingly, those whom I asked were usually those who were having a difficult day. No matter how bad a day they were having, no one would turn me down. I'm positive it was my charm.

There were hundreds of wonderful individuals who assisted me throughout each year of school, if only for a moment.

I remember one kid in particular. He was in my history class and had been paid as part of a program to take notes for me. Asking him his name, I smiled as I noticed him noticing my disability. After introducing myself, I asked him a little bit about his goals in life. He commented that he really didn't have any goals and then added that he hated school. "I'll put it to you this way," he said. "I'm here because my mom wants me here."

As our conversation went on, he told me about his mom and how she had passed away a few years previously. No one else in his family had gone to college. Before his mom died, he had promised her that he would break that cycle. I could see that he was depressed, and I understood why. I couldn't imagine how difficult it would be to lose my mom and to attend school if I didn't want to be there. I knew I had to ask him to help me so that God could somehow help him. Once class got out, I waited in the history department building for this gentleman to walk by. Once I spotted him, I pushed over to him and said, "I was wondering if you could help push me to my truck outside."

He stopped and looked around as if he were just seeing his surroundings for the first time, or possibly looking for an escape route. I waved with my hand, which is really more like a bear claw wave, since I can't move my fingers. I pretty much just raise my hand and move my forearm back and forth quickly, so it looks like my fingers are moving. I do it confidently, though, so it looks awesome instead of weird.

He paused for a moment before reluctantly responding, "Ummm, sure, I guess." A willing heart was all I needed. I explained to him how to grab my handles behind my wheelchair and push me, and off we went.

I shared with him my story as we made our way to my truck. He was surprised that I had not been in a wheelchair my entire life and also that as a youth I'd had a major head trauma.

"Dude, that stinks," he interrupted.

"Do you know what truly stinks?" I asked him.

"Ummm, being paralyzed?" he responded.

"Yes. Very much so," I said. "That and bad attitudes," I continued. "Bad breaks don't break good men," I told him. "In fact, with God's help, they will make you better."

As we arrived at my truck, I knew, as I had known with the BYU football team, that I had to show this individual how difficult it was for me just to get into my truck.

He wanted to help me, but I told him this single task had taken me a long time to master and proved what one can accomplish with a positive attitude and faith in yourself and God.

It took me twelve minutes to get into my truck.

After I was done, I could see that his soul had been softened and touched, as had mine. I told him his mom would be proud of him and let him know I'd see him in class the next week. After that incident, he'd often help me get to and from classes. Little did either of us know that asking for his help was about so much more than a simple push to and from class. God needed to let a struggling son know that He loved him and was aware of all he was carrying. I'm so grateful that God used me for His purpose, because that struggling son then turned around and became a huge blessing to me. When people ask where God is, the answer is simple: He's in you. It's simple: if you want God to do something to help others, then do something to help others.

Sometimes those who pushed me were reluctant and others were intimidating to ask, but no one ever turned me down. And then there were those who didn't wait for me to ask.

My mom often worried about me while I was going to college and prayed regularly that someone would be there to help me. A guy named Keith was the answer to her prayer and, subsequently, mine.

Keith and I were first years in the master of social work program. We had a few classes together and discovered we had a lot of the same interests. It didn't take us long to become friends. Often he would wait for me after class to push me to my next one, help grab books from my backpack, or get my lunch out of my bag without me even asking. He genuinely protected me. Giving me his number one day, Keith told me to call him anytime and for anything I needed.

The first time I texted Keith, he responded before I could even ask him for help. "The weather is bad," he wrote. "Text me when you get here, and I'll be right out."

This became a normal occurrence for Keith. Often I was running late. Consequently, Keith would miss some of his classes to get me to mine. During the winter, when I was in night school, my classes would get out late at night. Keith was adamant about getting me to my truck and making sure I made it inside safely every time. I'm sure he didn't realize that was one of my biggest fears. It would take very little for me to get stuck late at night on a patch of uneven ice, unable to push forward. If that were to happen with no one around, I'd be in big trouble. He was a lifesaver to me many times.

One rainy day, Keith was waiting for me early in the morning. We were in a rush, so he was pushing me a bit faster than usual. Though I am always grateful for people who serve me, I am also very apprehensive as well. I have to have a lot of faith in others. If bumps in the road aren't taken at the right angle or the right speed, my two front caster wheels will stop abruptly and can catapult me out.

Seeing an approaching bump that day, I cautioned Keith to slow down. Two seconds later, I went sailing through the air before coming to an abrupt stop with my face in the grass. Once I knew I was okay, I burst out laughing while Keith apologized profusely before quickly picking me up. With people passing us on all sides and while holding me in his arms, Keith joked, "You have no idea how long I've waited to cradle you in my arms." Both of us straight as an arrow, we laughed for quite a while as we continued to class.

Keith moved away after graduation, got married to a beautiful girl, and has two darling kids. We didn't know each other very long. We never hung out outside of school, and we haven't really talked since graduating. Our paths crossed briefly in this life, yet he treated me like a brother.

On TV, the news often depicts a divided people, a society of people constantly taking advantage of each other, fighting and self-serving. Yet I have seen firsthand how one truly receives what he or she gives out. If I react in kindness, I am often treated the same way. There are many who won't hesitate to go the extra mile in service of their fellow men. I had people of every skin color, religion, and nation helping me throughout my long eight years of school. As long as I was optimistically engaged and helping others, the blessings and the friendships that came my way because of it were miraculous. Never could I have imagined that my disability, the very thing that would make school so incredibly difficult for me, would end up giving me, and perhaps even some others, the greatest education.

The lowest grade I ever received while attending college was a B-, and I had a grade point average of 3.75, something that was completely foreign for me. I hardly ever paid personally for my schooling either. Every opportunity I had to apply for scholarships, I was amazingly and gratefully selected.

There is no doubt in my mind that the Lord blessed me with an increased ability to learn as well as provided me the resources necessary to continue my education. After successfully graduating with my associate's degree from Salt Lake Community College, I transferred to Weber State University for my bachelor of science degree.

I successfully graduated with a BA from Weber State University and found out through my schooling that I was pretty good at counseling and helping others. I guess you could call me the traveling counselor on wheels.

Wanting to help people overcome their own paralyzing trials in life, I was led straight toward applying for my master's degree at the University of Utah. Accepted into the social work program, I would attend the very college where Miss Davis, my counselor, had reluctantly told me I could not go because of poor grades. Now, six years later, they welcomed me with open arms.

Two years after being accepted into the social work program, I would graduate successfully with my master's degree.

To celebrate, I decided I would take my first solo ATV excursion up in the mountains, in a retrofitted four-by-four I had given myself as a graduation present. Weeks before I would start work at Intermountain Medical Center (IMC) as a social worker, I headed up to the hills of Bountiful for a day trip that would end up costing me my life. A stranger would bring me back again, as God would call me to live for the third time.

Chapter 14

LORD, HAVE MERCY ON THE FROZEN MAN

I was dying.

Suffering terribly both in body and spirit, I began to freeze to death. Helplessly suspended over a cold piece of ground, still strapped into my ATV and all alone, I hung in the mountains 9,500 feet above Bountiful. Fear started to creep in. With no one there to console or rescue me, I had power over nothing.

I had just pulled off the improbable: graduating with my master's degree. My friends in school all celebrated graduation in different ways; some went on trips while others bought themselves fancy graduation gifts. I chose to head to the mountains by myself where I feel close to my Savior. I wanted to go somewhere where I could reflect on my recent achievement and get a sense of what Heavenly Father wanted me to do next with my life. Six months prior to graduation, I began preparing for my solo day trip.

My dad had a side-by-side ATV that I was dying to drive. I yearned to go back to the beautiful Wasatch Mountains that I had spent so much time in as a youth. I missed the mountain range's beauty and vistas desperately. To make this a possibility, I purchased hand controls and power steering, which enabled me to drive my dad's side-by-side with my hands. To successfully get inside the ATV, I used a lift, which helped me transfer into the side-by-side with the help of two people. A five-point racing harness was used to keep me firmly upright and balanced in the driver's seat. The tightened straps served as my trunk stability, enabling me to drive. Next, I made the ATV street legal so that I could drive on the main roads leading up to the mountain trails roughly a mile and a half away.

Saturday, June 30, was a beautiful spring day. That morning my parents helped me transfer into the side-by-side before strapping me into my seat belt.

"Make sure you're back within three hours," my mom reminded me. "Your dad and I have a funeral to go to this afternoon." She handed me my binoculars, water bottle, and cell phone, which I strapped around my neck. I noted the look of concern in both my parents' eyes as I turned on the ATV.

Despite their reservations, they both understood that this was something I had to do on my own. Being almost thirty years old and still relying on my parents to do most things for me was a tough dynamic for both of us. We had to find places where I could have my own space and sense of freedom, even if only for a short time. Every so often, it became necessary to recharge my soul so that I could handle being dependent on my parents and others to live.

"Mom, I'll be fine," I said. "Don't worry about me. I'll be back in three hours. If anything happens, I'll call you. I love you guys," I finished, before opening the throttle and zooming down the street toward the mountains above.

Arriving at my destination, I began my ascent up the mountain. Thankfully, the dirt roads weren't dusty because we had received heavy rains a few days before. With temperatures unseasonably low, the weather was perfect.

I knew where I wanted to go. It had been over ten years since I had visited the Sheepherder Camp, nestled some 9,500 feet above Bountiful, at the top of Holbrook Canyon. I knew this place well. In high school, my friends and I would go hunting, four wheeling, and snowmobiling here often. I was eager to create new memories and reacquaint myself with the beauty of the landscape I had known intimately as a youth.

As I was driving, I noticed how incredible the mountains were. To me, they seemed greener and more colorful than I had ever remembered them appearing. With all the moisture we'd been receiving, the mountains were at their best. Streams gushed out of every spring and slot in the canyon, filling the mountainside with wildflowers. Beautiful aspen trees and alpine meadows made up the landscape high above me while the view of the valley grew more impressive the higher I climbed. With every blink of my eye, I captured a photo for my memory.

Occasionally, I'd stop the ATV to take in the beauty of the Lord's creations. I watched as people passed me by while I was pulled over. I'd nod a friendly hello and wave, though not understanding how people could simply drive up the mountain trail without ever stopping to look at the incredible scene surrounding them.

Often, when I am outside I spot the most magnificent bald eagles flying high above my house. Catching the canyon winds over the Wasatch Front, they glide down over the valley as if upheld by an invisible magic carpet. As I push my chair after them, I try to imagine the freedom they must truly enjoy.

A neighbor driving by my house once witnessed me outside, my head looking to the sky. Curious, he'd pulled over and asked me if I was okay. I said that I was doing great and was watching beautiful bald eagles hovering above our homes. Surprised, he said, "I've never seen an eagle around here before."

I replied, "Have you ever looked up?"

Pausing for a moment, he looked at me and smiled before quickly pulling into his driveway next door. A little while later, he reemerged with his wife and children. As they came running outside, I watched them look to the sky, finally seeing the hidden beauty that had always been there.

A quote attributed to Reginald Vincent Holmes says, "The earth has music for those who listen."[7]

Once I reached my desired destination, it felt like I was on top of the world. The views from this high mountain peak were spectacular. Turning off my ATV, I took it all in, soaking up the peace and serenity around me. My life was good today. I was amazed that I was actually driving the ATV on my own. Every breath I took filled my lungs with the fresh, cool aroma of pine trees and wildflowers. Truly happy, I was grateful that Heavenly Father enabled me to enjoy these surroundings.

Looking at the valley below, I reflected on how I had handled the difficulties in my life, first with my traumatic brain injury and then with my spinal cord injury. I was proud of myself for seeing God through my disability. I was so grateful for loving parents who cared for me, but more important, who taught me at a young age, through their example, to love the Lord with all my heart and to follow His teachings. I knew with a surety

---

7. *Fireside Fancies* (1955), 27.

that the Lord had preserved my life on multiple occasions, a knowledge that had enabled me for the most part to be happy and productive through my difficult trials. Feeling grateful that through the grace of God I was able to successfully graduate with my master's degree, I was excited about my future.

Saying a prayer of gratitude, I asked the Lord what the next chapter in my life should look like. I had already felt impressed to seek employment at the Intermountain Medical Center in Murray, Utah, and wanted to include the Lord in those plans. Everything came down to me passing the state social work exam that I would take in the next two months, and I was nervous.

Looking at my phone, I couldn't believe two hours had already passed. Three o'clock was fast approaching. I knew I couldn't be late, or my parents would miss their friend's funeral. In that moment, I distinctly remember thinking, *I have so much to be thankful for.* Then another thought followed, this one more random than the first: *I hope my parents never have to attend my funeral.*

I turned my ATV back on and started to turn around so that I could make the long descent back down the mountain and get home on time. Seeing a fork in the road at the bottom of the trail I was on, I then made a decision that changed my situation from one of serenity and peace to a living nightmare that still haunts me today.

I noticed the fork in the road led to two different paths. I knew the path on the right was safe and would lead me toward home. The path on the left went deeper into the woods. I was unsure where it would take me. Letting my ATV idle, I sat there momentarily as I decided which route I should take. I noticed a feeling that seemed to say, *Brandon, stay on the road that leads you home.*

I knew that if I went right, I would drive down the canyon. I would then easily and quickly get back home. However, I was tempted to try my luck with this new path, wondering where it may lead me. Foolishly, I chose the unfamiliar road.

At first, the trail was terrific with no obvious warning signs of danger below, but as I drove further, conditions suddenly deteriorated. Quickly the road became very steep and treacherous. Nervous now, I looked further down the path in front of me. I saw that it stopped abruptly with no place to turn around. It was a horrible dead-end trap. Immediately, I chided myself for taking this route, wondering how I was going to turn around and get back. As I was having these thoughts, I noticed a very light rain had begun to fall.

Crawling closer to the dead end below me, I saw that the slant of the road suddenly and dramatically sloped downward. This wasn't the first time this road had been traveled either. Visual tracks served as warning signs for me where others had turned around and tried to escape this path. Looking for a way out, I could see that there was just enough room for me to potentially turn around if I drove slightly off the dirt road. As I looked to the right side of my ATV just before the dead end, I noticed a large drop of about five hundred feet.

As if some unseen person could give me confidence and strength, and thinking these could be my last words, I yelled out, "Somebody help me! I'm turning around on top of a narrow cliff! This is crazy!"

The potential for disaster was huge. Tremendously apprehensive and using all the energy I could muster, I maneuvered the steering wheel while pushing on the gas. Somehow, I successfully turned the ATV around. Breathing a huge sigh of relief, I noted the visible cliff edge now on my left side. The sound of the creek rushed ominously below me. The only way that I could go back up the steep road I had come down was by opening the throttle quickly. Wanting nothing more than to leave the terrifying cliff behind me as quickly as possible, I pressed down hard on the gas pedal with my hand controls and began to make my escape. Halfway back up the hill—and just as I was breathing a sigh of relief—my ATV suddenly hit a large pine-tree root growing across the trail. Immediately my two front wheels jumped three feet in the air. The sudden impact threw my left hand off my handlebar, leaving me without access to both the gas and the brake.

"No, no, no!" I cried out.

With all my strength, I tried to get my hand back on the gas, but it was too late. The ATV instantly started to roll backward, gaining speed as it descended the narrow trail. My limited strength pressed the brake and the gas, but it wasn't enough to stop the momentum of the ATV. As I rolled backward, a million thoughts started to move through my mind.

Bracing for the worst, I knew that I would roll uncontrollably down the steep cliff, which would most assuredly end my life. The ATV suddenly and violently flipped over, landing on the driver's side, before sliding backward ten feet off the road. Waiting for the sudden drop, I heard two loud cracks before the ATV came to a complete stop.

It happened so quickly that I had to take a minute to recollect what had just happened. With a terrified laugh, I yelled, "I'm alive!"

A feeling of gratitude instantly hit me as I remembered stopping a gentleman I had seen four miles back and asking him if he'd mind helping me re-adjust my posture so that my body (especially my head) was again within the confines of the roll bar cage. If he hadn't helped me, the ATV would have crushed my head when it rolled.

Next I began to assess my injuries. Looking down toward my legs, I noticed a large wooden stump pressing firmly on my left knee and thigh. My original assumption was that the force of the impact from this wooden stump had probably broken my leg, but because I couldn't feel it, I wasn't sure.

Though I was surprised and grateful for the abrupt stop, I was now hanging parallel to the ground securely strapped in by my seat belt. Wondering what had stopped me from rolling off the cliff, to my great surprise, I noticed that a small aspen grove had caught the ATV. It was the only grouping of aspens that I had seen on the trail, and I had happened to roll into them. The cracking sound I had heard was a couple of the trees breaking as they held me fast in place. If it weren't for those trees, my body would have been found in the bottom of the canyon.

I also perceived that I was lucky in the way I'd rolled. If I had rolled three feet sooner, the wooden stump that now rested by my thigh would have smashed my head so severely that it would've killed me instantly. After realizing how lucky I had been in how everything had transpired and that I was still breathing, I quickly reached around my neck for my phone so that I could call for help.

Instantly panic struck. My hands desperately searched for the lanyard that my phone was attached to. It wasn't anywhere to be found. Using my arms to swing my body back and forth, I attempted to locate it. On my third attempt, I found it. Swinging back and forth again, I thought to myself, *I got you.* When I tried to grab it with my hands, my heart dropped. It was just out of reach.

The impact of the roll had ripped the lanyard from my neck and thrown it four feet away, just inches from my grasp. Without the ability to release myself from my extensive seatbelt, there was nothing I could do but stare at the phone longingly.

Realizing I needed to call on the only person who knew my predicament and could hear me, I prayed out loud and asked God to somehow lead someone to find me.

As I hung there, I berated myself. I was so disappointed that I had ignored the warning signs, including the feeling that had told me not to go down this road. Stupidly, I had taken an unfamiliar road, not knowing where it would lead. Foolishly distracted by the temptation of my surroundings and by the idea of what lay just around the bend, I was led into a trap. Now here I was, alone. As I hung there contemplating whether God would listen to my prayer after I had just ignored His warnings, my mind took me back to the moment where I stood in a courthouse before a judge, waiting to hear what my sentence would be.

It was just after Cameron and I had taken the snowmobiles for a joyride around town after a snowstorm. At the time, I thought what I had done was funny. I was proud of it, even parading my antics in front of all the kids at the high school. However, it turned out not to be so humorous when what started out as a thoughtless decision almost turned into a life-changing one.

"You understand, Brandon, that what you did was wrong and that you broke the law on multiple infractions," the judge said, sternly looking at me from behind his desk. "You took several officers on a high-speed chase through neighborhoods. Your escapade around Bountiful and the chase that ensued put not only you at risk but also the community, as well as law enforcement." The judge paused. "Because of that choice, you now have a criminal record and will be banned from getting a US visa."

Fear started to overcome me, bringing with it an immense feeling of regret and sadness. With the judge's words, he had just let me know that my number-one desire of serving a mission would now not be possible. Not only would I have a criminal record, but also without a visa, I would not be able to leave the United States. I had just blown my lifelong desire of serving my Heavenly Father with one single decision.

Panicked, I humbly responded, "Your honor, please . . . serving a mission is something that I have always wanted to do, ever since I was little. I've even worked hard my entire youth to save enough money to pay for it. I beg of you, please forgive me! I know what I did was wrong, and I'm willing to pay whatever price to make amends, but please don't keep me from serving my mission!"

Without pausing, the judge quickly replied, "You made that decision when you broke the law. You have no one to blame but yourself."

The pain in my shoulders brought me back to the present. The memory still fresh in my mind, sadness overcame me. How easy it would have been to avoid that situation when I was eighteen and this one over ten years later. The judge was right, and it was just as true today: I couldn't blame the ATV or the trail and its dangers; I could only blame myself.

As I lay with my head barely touching the dirt, the straps of my tightly fastened safety harness dug deep into my shoulders . . . the one place I could feel pain. As the blood started rushing toward my head, I began to yell, "Help! Can anybody hear me?! I need your help!"

My cries were met with silence and the cheerful chirping of the birds above, as if to say all was right in the world.

Chapter 15

SAVE ME

My love for everything outdoors started at a young age. Hours upon hours were spent exploring and enjoying the woods. I respected and loved being in God's natural playground. Always stopping, staring, and taking in the view or watching wildlife, I noticed my friends often didn't see what I did. God must have put a strong love of nature in me, knowing that much of my life would be spent watching. I am grateful that He did. Nothing screamed freedom for me like walking through the woods. Looking up to the mountains, pointing my finger, and choosing that day's destination was thrilling. The less-traveled the trail, the better.

In junior high, young men believe they're tough and independent, but they're still very naïve when it comes to thinking like responsible men. They start to grow a few whiskers and believe they are no longer boys.

Though most of my friends didn't have the passion for the outdoors that I had, what we did have in common was our mischievous ways. We all desired freedom. It was this that enabled me to sell the idea of a secret camping spot to my friends. I called it *Camp Russia*.

To be honest, I really don't remember why the name stuck, but it did—all the way through junior high and even high school. Maybe it was because of the movie *Red Dawn*. In it, America is invaded by Russia. The young men who escape in the film find shelter from capture in the woods.[8] Just like the men in the movie, we too found shelter from capture, not from the Russians but from a myriad of enemies that were always percolating through our imaginations.

Because I frequently explored the foothills of Bountiful, I oversaw finding the right location. It had to be off the beaten trail—secluded enough that no foot traffic would ever find it, yet close enough to civilization that we could act out our mischievous tasks. We had to have a clear visual advantage, a spot large enough to house two to three tents (complete with fire pit and benches), and brush thick enough to hide our campfires at night. It didn't take me long to find the perfect spot.

The ideal location was no more than a quarter mile off Bountiful Boulevard and halfway up the mountain, near a spring we used to fill up our water purifiers. Camping backpacks would be used to cart necessities, like food, to and from Camp Russia. Meals of choice included anything we could find from our parents' cupboards: cans of beef stew, Cup Noodles, and a few granola bars. Camp Russia soon became our second home.

In between classes at school I'd walk the halls, and like a spy on a mission, I'd whisper to my friends, "Meet me tonight at Russia." No one outside our group knew what we were talking about. At the appointed time, we'd emerge from

---

8. *Red Dawn*, directed by John Milius (1984; MGM/UA Entertainment Company).

our individual homes and make our way to Russia's fortress, where we immediately set to work planning strategies for that evening's adventures. The freedom of shooting our .22s in the woods, joking and laughing about friends, and talking about girls and sports was a big part of Camp Russia.

Some of our "greatest" ideas came from Camp Russia hangouts, like "fishing for cars and hanging them." After dinner, empty beef stew cans were collected. We'd string them together on both ends of a long piece of fishing line from my tackle box. After making our way down to the road below, we'd hide on opposite sides of the road. We would drape the fishing line across, with the cans on each side, and wait for a car to drive by and snatch it out of our hands. Our single goal was to hold the nearly invisible fishing line high enough that the car's grill would grab it and drag the cans behind the car like newlyweds announcing their nuptials.

Laughing hysterically at the scene, we'd watch as our contraptions were sometimes dragged over a block before they were noticed. Because the noise was so loud, it usually didn't take long for drivers to pull over and remove the fishing line. Once they did, we'd quickly run over and recover the stringed cans before setting up our trap again. Oftentimes the same car we'd just canned would drive back around to see if they could spot who was doing the "canning." Ultimately, they'd get canned again, only this time at a different spot on the same road. The driver would usually get so agitated and embarrassed at getting caught for a second time that they wouldn't even bother getting out, instead choosing to drive until the line fell off or broke.

One night we happened to accidentally can a cop car driving by. I was so dumbstruck that it nearly incapacitated me, preventing me from running away. Gathering what adrenaline I had, I screamed my warning as loud as I could, "Run to Russia! Run to Russia!"

Camp Russia holds a special place in my heart. It is filled with emotions, memories, friends, and thoughts that have long since evaporated into silence mingled with longing to be reunited with that boy and his hideout. The place I had loved and often played at as a youth was less than a mile from where I now lay trapped.

My eyes suddenly flew open.

I cried out as burning pain struck me repeatedly.

Looking at the ground to find the source of the pain, I quickly caught sight of the culprits. To my horror, I had rolled over and demolished a giant red-ant hill. By the looks of it, the ants were not pleased. Hundreds of them had already begun crawling all over my head and body and the ATV. I began swatting at them over and over as they bit me. In disbelief and incredible pain, not only from the ants but also from the amount of time I had already spent hanging upside down, I looked up at the sky and cried out, "Seriously?!"

As if in response, the winds picked up, bringing darker clouds over the mountaintops. The air had turned noticeably cooler, and in the distance I could hear thunder. Shaking my head in disgust, I thought, *Really, Lord?* In the back of my mind, the feeling of impending doom settled. Completely stuck, I could not even brush the ants from my hair.

Two hours passed with nobody coming down the road to save me. Rain that was quickly turning to sleet had begun to pour down on me. Dressed in nothing but shorts and a T-shirt with a thin black vest over the top, I could feel my core body temperature slowly starting to drop. In response, my body began to shake uncontrollably.

Fighting the growing fear inside of me, I tried not to think about the worst that could happen. If I allowed myself to go there, it wouldn't be long before I would become irrational, making my situation worse. The only way that I could last until help arrived was to keep my mind focused and positive. I began to put my mind in survivor mode. Deciding to concentrate on what I could control, I started to sing hymns to calm my mind.

"Be still, my soul: The Lord is on thy side," I began. "With patience bear thy cross of grief or pain. Leave to thy God to order and provide." Emotion caught in my throat. "In ev'ry change he faithful will remain." I began to feel encouraged and hopeful as I sang. "Be still, my soul: Thy best, thy heav'nly Friend thru thorny ways leads to a joyful end." As the winds picked up, so did my singing. "Be still, my soul: Thy God doth undertake to guide the future as he has the past. Thy hope, thy confidence let nothing shake; all now mysterious shall be bright at last." The wind continued to swirl around me as I finished. "Be still, my soul: The waves and winds still know his voice who ruled them while he dwelt below."[9]

Though the wind and rain was causing me to grow colder, it washed the ants off of me, and for the moment I was grateful for it. Continuing to sing hymn after hymn, I pictured in my mind the powerful Tabernacle Choir singing by my side, their voices lending me strength. My soul filled with energy and hope, briefly blocking out the circumstance I was in. Still, I knew I had very little time to be rescued. The longer I was exposed to the elements, the harder my body and mental state

9. "Be Still, My Soul," text by Katharina Von Schlegel, translated by Jane Borthwick, 1752; music by Jean Sibelius, 1900.

would be tested. I knew both the best-case scenario and the worst-case scenario. Trying to remain positive, I prayed constantly for my Heavenly Father to give me the strength necessary for either outcome. If I could at least hold out until search and rescue arrived . . .

It seemed that every time I tried to be optimistic, the elements fought back. I felt as though I were standing in a freezer with wet clothes on, and the shock of the cold temperature took my body to the most painful extremes I had ever felt. With winds and freezing rain constantly beating down on me and hours continuing to pass, my blood eventually stopped flowing to my lower extremities.

I was freezing to death, and I knew it.

As my entire body became numb, every raindrop felt like ice pelting me.

My eyes opened with some effort. For a moment, I couldn't grasp what was happening. *Where am I? Did I pass out? Am I unconscious? Is that the first time? How long have I been hanging here?* Coherent and incoherent thoughts moved through my mind before settling on my family. I began to think about their reactions when they realized something had happened to me. Fear and worry would consume them. The sudden awareness that my parents would miss the funeral they were supposed to attend to come look for my body was agonizing. I remembered my last thought as I had left their house that morning. *I hope they don't ever have to attend my funeral.* My fear intensified as I realized that the thought had been foreshadowing.

My family would have no clue where to find me. Thinking of their panic and worry and all I had put them through was overwhelming. My heart ached. I realized how foolish a thing it is to die doing something you love, something that could ultimately take you away from those you love. Over and over I wished that I had not gone down this risky path. Tears began to fall from my eyes as an apologetic mantra cried out from my lips for a family that could not hear me and who would never know how truly sorry I was.

Being the oldest, I was my siblings' physical and emotional protector. I held every one of them when they were little and cared for them. I tried to be a big brother who was always there. After my neck injury, the roles suddenly reversed. They were now my protectors in storms I could not fight. I relied upon their physical strength and support. They had come through for me repeatedly, but they each also carried emotional scars from all I had put them through.

Only eight years old at the time of my second accident, Bridgett, or Gidge, as we all lovingly call her, had stomach issues and suffered from anxiety. While my mom worked full time to help pay for my many medical needs, Gidge became my arms and legs, grabbing things I couldn't reach. She was now the one making me meals, as I had once done for her. As the years passed and we both became adults, she never stopped serving me.

Brittney, just a few years older than Gidge, would literally take on the role of my nurse. While I was in the hospital after my neck injury, and while watching the various healthcare professionals lend me aide, she determined to become a nurse practitioner. Starting her schooling before she had even graduated from high school, Brittney would become the youngest nurse case manager at Primary Children's hospital. Though I had taken so much attention and time away from her during her youth, she continued to unselfishly give me more of it.

Only a year and a half younger than me, Bronson was the other half of my heart, brain, body, and soul. From the very first injury, Bronson had been there pushing me, counseling me, protecting me, and lifting me. There isn't anything Bronson wouldn't give up or do if I needed it. Bronson is the first person I call, the first to arrive on scene, and the last to leave.

Knowing my siblings were out searching in this horrid storm for their lost, helpless big brother tore at my heart. After my neck injury, they'd often say, "We will always have your back like you had ours. We will always protect you." They had kept their promise while I had broken mine. Putting myself in this situation put them right back to square one.

It hit me with full force that there was a strong possibility I would never see them again while alive. Overwhelming sorrow and heartache coursed through my soul. Mountains that were once my greatest escape and biggest blessing had betrayed me. I had hastily and selfishly made a decision that didn't affect only me, and now because of it I was not the only one suffering in that moment. This solo trip to prove my independence had come at too great a cost.

By the fourth hour of hanging upside down, my body's capacity to withstand the pain was spent. The rain and cold were absolutely destroying my outer body, which appeared completely pale and blue now. It was then that the pain shifted. Hours before, it was felt primarily on the outside of my body, and now, like a disease bent on destroying its host, it worked its way inward. Violent shaking had racked my body in its desperate attempts to stay warm, and now there was only eerie stillness, a physical sign that my body had admitted defeat and stopped its attempts to save my life. It was only a matter of time.

In this moment of torture and horrific realization, I panicked. Immediately a desire to quickly end my pain took over. I rationalized that I would take one last breath, hold it in, and never breathe again.

Sucking in every bit of oxygen I could carry in my lungs, I held my breath and waited to die. For what seemed like five minutes I refused to release my breath, the burning in my lungs no match for the pain I was already in. I could feel myself getting close to losing consciousness. Death was closing in. Soon I would never need to breathe again. As I began to drift away, I heard a soft and calm voice whispering inside of me.

"Brandon, breathe . . . Brandon, breathe."

Still holding my breath, I heard the voice lovingly and quietly say, "This is not your decision. It is mine. I'll be the one who decides when and where you'll be called home."

As the words were spoken, warmth radiated from within my soul, bringing with it an increased energy to open my eyes and breathe again.

I obeyed.

For the next ten minutes, I fought to catch my breath and feed my oxygen-deprived body. I knew from the voice that dying was not my choice to make. Determined now, I vowed to hold on as long as I could, regardless of all I was feeling.

Another hour passed, and with my tongue now numb and swollen, I could barely swallow the endless trickle of water that flowed into my mouth. Internally, terrible cramps and sharp pains moved through my vital organs.

The fifth hour, slipping in and out of consciousness, I noticed that the sores from my shoulder harness hurt less and less. My heart struggled to pump blood through my cold veins. Dazed and confused, and losing consciousness for minutes at a time now, I would quickly realize that I had stopped breathing.

I started to feel my muscles in my body become stiff, which made it nearly impossible to raise and extend my arms. I felt my heart pulse as it progressively moved slower and slower. Breathing became extremely painful and difficult.

When death approaches, you begin to relive every moment in your life. As I recalled mistakes I had made, both big and small, I pleaded with the energy of my soul to be forgiven so that I might enter God's paradise and eventually receive the gift that I so desperately wanted: eternal life with a perfect body.

Looking for strength within, I understood that though my body was dying, my soul was ageless. It had been created to withstand and understand this difficult journey that we all must pass through. I understood that when I died, eventually I would be resurrected again and brought to stand before God to be judged of the works I had performed in this life. As my eyes began to fade to darkness again, a scripture came to my mind, bringing with it the rest of a memory: "For all have sinned, and come short of the glory of God" (Romans 3:23).

I was back in front of the judge after my snowmobile incident and had just finished pleading for mercy. I waited with bated breath for the words that would come out of his mouth and determine my future. He had just returned from making his final decision about my case.

"Brandon," he began, "from your record, I can tell that you are a good person." He paused. "Also that you are truly sorry for what you did."

A spark of hope began to flicker inside of me.

"If you abide by what will be required of you to fulfill," the judge continued, "your record will be clean and erased."

Utterly elated, I wanted to cry out. In an instant, the substantial weight that had previously rested on my shoulders was now gone. Emotion filled me with excitement as gratitude coursed through me.

The judge ended with a warning. "But if not, justice will stand, and so will your criminal record."

I felt like I could fly home. I had just been given a second chance. Though I had to pay a consequence, the judgment was fair and merciful, and if I did my part, I would be rewarded with a clean slate.

I was given 250 hours of community service that day. In my mind, it was a small price to pay. I worked those hours off quickly and without complaint. Never again was anything going to keep me from fulfilling my mission. Wherever the Lord decided to call me, I would go.

Tears rolled down my cheeks as I contemplated what it would feel like to stand before God at the mercy seat and be judged of my sins. Would my elation be the same as it was when I stood before the judge over a decade previously? Would gratitude and awe course through me at this impossible gift that my Savior had made possible? Would I even be able to stand as I comprehended His sacrifice, while at the same time having a perfect knowledge of all my sins that not only led to that very sacrifice but also made it necessary?

I thought of the various awful physical and mental pains Christ must've endured while in the Garden of Gethsemane and on the cross. I took comfort in knowing that the Lord knew what it felt like to experience what I was going through at this very moment. Once again, I began to pray, but this time it was different.

"Father in Heaven," I began, "I'm thankful for the life that Thou hast given me. I've been blessed richly with great parents and wonderful siblings. Please bless them. Give them peace and assurance that I'll be in a better place. Father, I understand that I will not be rescued. Please forgive me for my weaknesses and for any bad decisions made in mortality." I paused. There were no more tears to cry, but a strong spirit flowed through me. When I had first become stuck, I asked my Heavenly Father to send someone to save me. Now I understood that He already had. Someone had been sent to save us all.

This time I did not pray to be physically saved.

"Please God," I finished, "save me, with Thee in Thy kingdom. In the name of Jesus Christ, amen."

Through glazed eyes, I looked and waited for my deceased grandparents to come and take my hand, telling me that it was time to go home.

The last moment I can recall that day was taking a deep breath before shouting, "Father, take me or save me! I cannot hold on any longer!"

And then I was gone.

Chapter 16

I'M ALIVE?

I lay unresponsive in a deep coma in the ICU unit of Lakeview Hospital in Bountiful, Utah. My dad was frantically stating to the many nurses and doctors that he needed to give me a blessing. The medical staff explained that it would be extremely dangerous for my heart, which was barely beating as it was; even the slightest touch could put stress on it. It had stopped its fight while I was up on the mountain and had only begun to beat again after the search and rescue team administered CPR hours previously.

Because of the concerns of warm hands shocking my cold head, family members instead opted to place their hands on my covered body to bless me.

My sister Brittney stood watching everything unfold, understanding better than all of us the realities of what we were facing. With her medical expertise, she explained to my family that I would not survive. The hypothermia was too severe. Bringing a body back to its proper temperature is a delicate process. That is often when those affected by the extreme cold ultimately pass away, due to the stress their body is put through.

Miraculously, as my body was slowly and meticulously warmed back up, I remained stable. With each increasing degree of warmth, the hope of the medical team and my family rose. Once my core temperature was in the eighties, my doctors decided to risk moving me, as it was my only hope of recovery.

For the second time in my life, I was transferred from Lakeview Hospital in my hometown to IMC Hospital in Salt Lake City, where their trauma one unit would have the resources and expertise to bring me back to life.

I was wrapped in a three-inch-thick blanket that was warming me both inside and out while a circulatory system of tubes moved warm water through the chamber that encased me. In the wintertime, as kids we used to dare each other to run outside through the snow with bare feet. Sometimes we'd even roll in it while wearing a swimsuit before running to a bubbling hot tub and hopping in while still covered in snow. There were always a few seconds of burning as bodies that were too cold were shocked by the two extreme temperatures. For this same reason, someone with hypothermia must be warmed very slowly. Each hour, my body temperature was raised only one degree, so as not to elicit any type of nerve response that would cause my body to fight pain or be overworked in any way. The process was carefully monitored. I was administered propofol through a machine to keep me asleep through the process. It was the same anesthesia that Michael Jackson used to come in and out of sleep and would die from that very week.[10]

Like a light switch, once the medicine is turned off, the patient instantly awakens. Conversely, once it turns on, consciousness is immediately lost.

---

10. "Death of Michael Jackson," *Wikipedia: The Free Encyclopedia*, last modified Jan. 31, 03:57, https://en.wikipedia.org/wiki/Death_of_Michael_Jackson.

One of my church leaders, who also happened to be a dear family friend and neighbor, had come to offer peace to my family and stay by their side. Wanting to get a better understanding as to whether he was there to lend peace to a family whose son was about to die or to give encouragement that I would live, he asked one of my doctors what my chances truly were for survival.

The doctor remarked that he had never worked on a patient with a core temperature as cold as mine, but he felt the true reading would be whether I responded when the propofol was turned off. Pausing, the doctor then turned to my neighbor. "In fact," he said, "why don't we try that right now?"

My neighbor watched as the doctor walked over to the machine administering the propofol to my body. He then flipped the switch. Described as a Lazarus moment, though I had been once dead, I was instantly back. My eyes shot open. Terrified, I looked around the room before my whole body began to shake. My neighbor yelled for someone to grab my parents.

As they ran into the room and began to console me, my countenance immediately softened.

The doctor spoke. "Let's put him back under," he said before flipping the switch again. Instantly I was out cold. The doctor then smiled. For the first time in two days, he said, "I think this is going to have a hopeful ending."

A loud clap startled me. I felt my body jump in response before somebody called my name.

"Brandon, you're at IMC Hospital. Can you hear me?" he asked before clapping his hands together again. "I need to make sure your brain is understanding me. Can you hear me?"

Although I was completely alert, confusion filled me.

I'm alive?

The doctor repeated what he had previously said.

"Yes," I whispered. "Yes. I can hear you."

I frantically searched for my family within my hospital room. Sorrow poured through me at the thought of what they must've endured. I didn't know if they were the ones who had found me, what state I had been in, and if they had been told that I was dead. All I knew was that I was not supposed to be here. I had died. Yet here I was.

When I'd gone through my last two major accidents, I had been present. I had seen my family go through grief, hardship, and stress as well as the pain that they each personally bore. Now I had done it to them again. The doctor, noticing my growing anxiety, moved to my side.

"Don't worry, Brandon," he said calmly. "You've done amazingly well with your recovery. Your family is here. In fact," he said with a smile, "I'm sure they'll love to hear from you." Searching his pockets, he located his cell phone and then pushed a couple of buttons and waited for my parents to answer his call.

I could tell by the tone of his voice and by the looks of the other hospital staff present that they were all amazed I was alive. Things were happening incredibly fast. Only a day and half had passed since I had died on the mountain. Now here I was awake and alive in a hospital room surrounded by people telling me I was a miracle.

Handing me his cell phone, the doctor said, "It's your mom."

Sorrow filled me once again. Taking the phone, I spoke quickly into it. "Mom and Dad, I'm so sorry. I'm so sorry. Please forgive me," I begged.

My mom was clearly in shock. "You're alive?" she said. "This is really Brandon?" She paused briefly. "Dad and I are downstairs in the cafeteria. We'll be right up as quick as we can!"

After the phone call, I had a million questions. What day was it? Had I been in a coma for days? Months? Years? Who had found me? What had happened after they found me? How did my parents know that I was here in the hospital? All the thoughts flooded my mind at once.

I looked down at my body as if aware of it for the first time. I noticed a few cuts and bloody scrapes on my arms and fingers. Areas on my arm where I do have some feeling were noticeably sore. The left side of my body, especially where the seatbelt straps had dug into my shoulder, was extremely numb. Although I was thrilled to be alive, losing any more feeling in my body is always a concern.

As a doctor came near my bedside, I hurriedly asked him if I was okay and told him about the numbness on my left side. The doctor gently reassured me. "You appear to be doing amazingly well, considering where you came from." He paused. "When they found you, Brandon, you had a reported body temperature of 73 degrees. As you know, normal is about 98.6."

Although I didn't understand how dangerous that was, I knew that getting a fever of only eight degrees higher could be deadly for the human body; surely going the other way twenty-five degrees was not survivable.

As if in response he said, "No one walks away—or in your case, rolls away—from 73 degrees."

I tried to process what he was telling me as he continued.

"Your recovery will be written about in medical journals for years and years to come. That's how unique it is. I've not heard of anyone ever coming back to life after having that low of a core temperature, but somehow you have, and even more remarkable is how well you are doing."

The sound of my parents rushing into my room interrupted our conversation. They looked at me, shocked that I was alive.

When the doctor had used his cell phone to call my mom to tell her that someone needed to talk to me, my mom was petrified that the crisis worker was calling to tell her that I had died.

"It was like hearing somebody speak from the dead when you called," she said, wide eyed. "At first, I couldn't even believe what I was hearing." She then explained to me that when she had sat by my hospital bed the day before and reached to take hold of my arm, she had quickly retracted, astonished at what she had felt. "It felt like I had opened the freezer section of the grocery store and pulled out some frozen hamburger," she said. Her eyes were round and full of bewilderment as she tried to convey to me what she had felt. "There was absolutely no give whatsoever when I pressed on your arm. You were dead."

As the realization began to set in, my mom quickly called my brother and sisters. I spoke to each of them, apologizing as I had done with my parents for putting them through yet another heart-wrenching accident, something that they were becoming all too accustomed to. All of them were absolutely stunned to hear my voice. They all thought they would be planning their brother's funeral in the days to come. After the phone calls were made, my siblings drove to the hospital to see this miracle with their own eyes, to reassure themselves that what they were hearing was, in fact, reality.

Only a few hours later, the psychological effects of what had happened to me were starting to replay themselves in my mind. Bronson slept by my side that night to provide comfort. Even after I returned from the hospital a mere two days after my accident, I found that I could not sleep alone. For the next

166

few nights, family members alternated sleeping on the couch in my room.

Very little scares me anymore. The most absolutely frightening sensation I have ever experienced was feeling my body slowly die with all its agonizing pains and then suddenly waking up alive in a hospital room filled with horrific memories. The comfort of my family kept me grounded as I tried to take my mind off reliving the nightmare I had experienced.

A week and a half later, I had the opportunity to go with my parents to personally thank those individuals from the search and rescue unit of Davis County who had found me. They were the literal answers to my fervent prayers that day on the mountain. My parents had a beautiful plaque made with my rescue date and the story of how these men and women had brought me back to life. In addition, we brought pastries to thank them for the "sweet" rescue.

Brandon and the members of the Davis County Search and Rescue team

I then was able to address the group and tell them what had transpired before they'd found me. With all the heartfelt gratitude I could give, I thanked each of them for taking time out of their busy Saturdays, for dropping everything they had planned that day to strap on their equipment and make finding me their number one priority. Not one of these individuals is paid for their service. They volunteer out of love for their fellow man and the outdoors.

After I was done speaking about what had gotten me into the situation, they each began to recount how they had gotten me out. Each rescuer came up and shook my hand before telling me his or her side of the story. Each person's account was remarkable, but there was one gentleman whose experience I was not prepared to hear.

The man was completely caught up in the moment when it was his turn to greet me. It was easy to see that he was struggling to keep his emotions in check. Overcome, he finally spoke. "When we found you, we could not get a pulse from you," he began. "We tried several times and at various locations on your body, but there was no heartbeat."

The man attempted to regain composure as the memories of that day came back to him. "We began to take off your wet clothes. You were absolutely freezing to the touch. Immediately an overwhelming feeling within me told me to say a sacred prayer and blessing in your behalf, you clearly having already passed on. So I did. Shortly thereafter, and to our amazement, your pulse came back. We knew we had just experienced a miracle."

Not having known any of this had taken place, I was absolutely blown away by what this gentleman was telling me. The very reason he had joined the Davis County search and rescue team was in hopes of one day saving someone's life. Tears filled my own eyes as I thanked him for acting on his impression from the Spirit and being the type of person living worthily so that he might be able to fulfill that prompting.

As I continued to talk with the other men and women, I started to realize that my rescue was no easy task. A man named Jason explained to me that they were just about to call off the search. Time was passing fast, and the conditions on the mountain made the likelihood of finding me alive very low.

Jason explained that in that moment he had an overwhelming impression to go down a road that he had passed earlier. He said, "I've never had an experience like this before. I'm not spiritual, but there is no other way to explain what I felt." He continued, "Reluctantly, I followed this impression down a very steep, wet dirt road. After going about twenty yards down the road, I found you!" he said. "However, I started to get really nervous. I didn't know what I would find as I looked around the ATV, but there you were, unresponsive, very cold, and pale."

Bewildered at the other side of my story, I was then told that it took seven gentlemen to carry me some one thousand yards up steep and wet dirt roads. It took extreme efforts on their part to get me to a place where a helicopter could land.

When they had first called in Life Flight, the helicopter pilot had tried to land twice but was unable to do so, due to the extreme weather and thunderstorms. There were dangerously high crosswinds that would literally suck all the power from the helicopter, hindering its ability to land. The rescue personnel stationed on the ground and waiting for the helicopter later told me that they knew driving me from where I was to the base of the mountain where their search and rescue headquarters was set up would kill me. The added stress of moving me in those conditions, on a body that was already lifeless, would have been just enough to send me into instant cardiac arrest. In order to save my life, they had to find a helicopter and pilot that could somehow land on the mountaintop in horrible weather conditions.

Life Flight was unsuccessful in their attempts, so one of the head search and rescue dispatchers decided to call the highway patrol to see if they could use their helicopter to help. They instantly agreed and located a very experienced older Vietnam War pilot who had flown for the highway patrol for many years.

The man recounting the story to me said the vet replied, "Okay, boys, let Life Flight try to land their bird one more time. If they can't, then I'll fly there and land my bird as quick as I can."

When Life Flight was unsuccessful again, this experienced pilot weaved in and out of the dangerous thunderstorm and landed his helicopter right on the spot needed to get my body to safety, but that wasn't the end of the dilemma.

Once the helicopter landed, rescuers immediately noticed that the highway patrol helicopter was a very small, albeit strong, helicopter that only had room for two—and one of those two had to be flying the chopper. My 6'2" frame posed a major problem for a helicopter not equipped for taking a passenger lying down. Getting me in the helicopter and securely fastened in while I was unconscious was going to be tricky. They were only able to fit my upper body in the chopper if my lower body dangled out the side door. With my upper body fastened inside, the helicopter pilot held on to me while flying, making sure I didn't fall out the other side!

My eyes must've gone pretty wide when I heard that.

"It's a good thing you weren't awake," Jason said in response. "Because that would've been one scary ride."

After hearing about many other miracles that had taken place in my rescue, it was confirmed to me yet again that life is not happenstance, nor is it equal. Each of us has a very individual plan. That's why it has to be okay that life is not fair and why trust in a Supreme Being who knows the big picture is crucial. He knows when to close doors and open others.

A month after my accident, I took the state exam that I had been worried about when I left on my solo ATV day trip. I passed that exam right before the window closed on a job vacancy I was applying for. When I had first gotten to the top of the mountain, I had asked God if working at IMC was the right path for me. While I was looking at the view below, images of me working at IMC's neuro-rehab facility had come to my mind. I could see myself teaching and counseling individuals who'd had life-changing accidents similar to mine. Excitement grew inside of me as I looked out over the valley that day. I knew IMC was the right place for me. Two weeks after leaving IMC as a patient, I would enter it again as an employee.

Chapter 17

BITTER OR BETTER

Ofttimes the test of courage
becomes rather to live than to die.[11]

—Vittorio Alfieri

The opportunity of working at IMC did not fall in my lap.

In the second year of my master's program, I had to complete a practicum of six hundred hours of supervised field training. Seated in class one day, I had just been handed a list of places where I could obtain those hours. As I scanned the list, none of the available options stood out to me. After praying for guidance and finally knowing what I wanted to do, I was disheartened not to find anything that fit my desires.

When I was growing up, my mom often said to her children, "If you don't like the outcome you see, then make the right one appear."

So I determined I would create my own practicum. I knew I wanted to work at IMC. Now I just had to make it happen.

---

11. Vittorio Alfieri, *Oreste*, 4.2.

Calling the director of the rehab facility at IMC, I set up an appointment with him for later that afternoon.

When I arrived, the director remembered me from years past. After we had gotten reacquainted, I jumped right in.

"I find it interesting that this great neuro-rehab facility doesn't have a single person in a wheelchair employed here. Your goal is to help injured patients return back home and become active members in society," I continued. "Wouldn't it be great to have someone working on this floor who is living proof of that achievement?"

The director smiled at me, knowing exactly what I was getting at.

Seeing that I now had him where I wanted him, I spoke boldly. "Here's what I think," I said confidently. "You guys need somebody working on this great unit who's not only been a patient but has gone through your rehab process." I smiled at him. "I am IMC's personal success story."

The director smiled back at me. "Brandon, you were one of our greatest patients," he said. "It would be an honor to have you working on this floor with us, but there are currently no job openings."

Undeterred, I knew that once they saw me interacting with the patients, they would understand that my role would be unique and valuable to their program, as well as the patients I counseled, and that ultimately they would create a space for me by the end of my six hundred hours. I just needed the director on board. "Since there isn't a job opening now," I said. "Can you do me a favor?"

"What's that?" he responded.

"Allow me to serve my second-year practicum underneath the head social worker on the unit," I said.

The director looked at me excitedly. "I'll make that happen," he replied.

It wasn't long after that meeting that I again entered IMC, but this time as a certified social worker.

Brandon beginning work at IMC Hospital

Since I couldn't write, all my patient assessments had to be recorded. Afterward, I would return to my office, where I'd put on a headset and replay the conversations I'd just had. I would then dictate to the computer what I was hearing, which then translated those conversations to text. For the casual person walking by, I probably looked like an air traffic controller, voicing out commands while looking at the computer. It always took me at least three times as long as an able-bodied person to do the same job. However, I couldn't let that get to me and be successful at the same time. I made sure that I excelled and worked harder than any able-bodied person could, and with a smile.

By the end of my six hundred hours, the gentleman I worked underneath decided to retire. As it turned out, there *was* a job opening on the unit, and it was waiting just for me. I thanked the Lord for guiding me toward this path of employment, for His goodness and mercy. It was another testament that God does direct our paths. Sometimes the outcome we want just isn't available at the time we are seeking it. Taking a step into the dark and being willing to work hard until that outcome becomes available enables God to work with time frames we don't control.

At a young age, after my head accident, was the first time that I learned that there will always come a time in life when everyone will face something both trying and inescapable. Whatever the trial—the death of a loved one, an unfavorable medical diagnosis, the effects of a poor decision made, a mental or physical disability, an addiction, economic challenges, and so on—at some point, we will all be taken to the very limits of our capacity to cope and live through these life-altering changes. Every day while working at IMC, I had a front row seat to people dealing with at least one of these trials. Not only that, but I could see how discouraged they felt, feeling like there was no one else who understood what they were going through.

One of the neatest things I witnessed while working on that unit was how a patient's face would fill with relief when they saw me roll into their room. All it took was one look at me in a wheelchair for them to instantly know that I knew what it was to face a great challenge. All it took for me to feel needed was their look of relief upon seeing me. For the first time in a long time, I was the asset. A person that you avert your eyes from on the street one day may become your biggest ally the next as we navigate a very unpredictable life. What a miracle and blessing it is for me to be able to offer someone hope and a visual of that hope in practice.

However, one of the biggest challenges I faced with patients who had just experienced a major life setback was how quickly they allowed fear to alter the very essence of who they were. Fear could literally destroy all sense of faith and purpose in someone's life. I held the hands of many patients and family members wanting to end their lives. I knew the feeling well. There were those who feared living as they were given life sentences of severe pain and hardship. In contrast, I witnessed patients who were given terminal diagnoses and saw their fear of dying. While one desperately wanted to live, another hoped to die. Each received the other's wish.

With either diagnosis, many patients developed a condition I called "It's All Over Syndrome." The first step was always fear. If fear goes unchecked, it can destroy us from the inside. The greatest battles we face in life are first fought within our souls. If we lose those battles, we lose everything.

I would often get a call from the intensive care unit of the hospital asking if I could help change a patient's desire to give up and instead help them fight off the chains of sorrow and hopelessness. I remember receiving one such call from an anxious social worker on the intensive care unit, asking me if I could help a man who had recently become paralyzed.

Saying a quick prayer, as I always did before entering a patient's room, I hoped that I could somehow be a bright light amongst the darkness that now filled him. Rolling into his room, I saw his parents in the corner, a look of desperation filling both their faces. The man was lying there struggling to breathe with the support of a machine. His SCI was both higher and more severe than mine; still I had been told by the nursing staff that there was hope that this young man could one day be as mobile as me.

As I took hold of his hand, it was hard not to see myself in this human being. I knew what he was telling himself. His vacant expression and blatant attempts not to acknowledge me led me to understand he would not be here much longer. When one is at that point, it becomes entirely necessary to fight to live. Pleading for him to not give up and to hold on, I said, "You have more capacity to live and progress than you think. Please don't decide to forgo an opportunity to live."

Unresponsive to my pleadings and past the point of return, he had clearly already made his decision. He stared at the ceiling as I continued. "With God's help, you will be blessed beyond what you can fathom if you choose to live. I will help you. Just don't give up. You still have so much you can do in your life."

His parents were openly crying now. My own tears fell as I understood that I could not change a mind already set on dying. Knowing this was the case, I simply said, "May God be with you until we meet again, my friend."

Later that evening, he passed away.

I struggled in those moments. I knew all too well that could have easily been me a decade before, while trying to decide if I could live this new life.

I am always sad about someone choosing to die, though I can understand his or her pain. Sometimes I, too, wish that I could be done with this life. I'd love to live pain free and without the confinement of my wheelchair; however, I know that isn't my decision to make. I felt bad for those I witnessed take a most sacred decision out of their Heavenly Father's hands. Perhaps the positive impacts that could've been made through their examples, along with the growth they would've experienced, was the very purpose for the trial in the first place.

Although every day of my life I find myself wishing I hadn't been through any one of my accidents, it is clear to me that the bulk of who I am is the result of those very incidents I'd wish away.

Unfortunately, the experience like the one I'd had with the man in the ICU was not the only time I'd be called on to help someone who chose not to fight.

A fellow therapist phoned me one afternoon, asking me if he and the father of one of his patients could meet with me. This was not uncommon. Because I was in a wheelchair, therapists who felt like they were not reaching a paralyzed patient would sometimes call. This time the patient was a man named Jake. He'd been in an accident that resulted in him becoming paraplegic. Father, son, and therapist all knew the situation was desperate, but only two of them cared.

A few days later, I met with Jake's dad. I could see the fear in this father's eyes and hear the pleading in his voice.

"Brandon, my son is dying," Jake's dad said before he'd even sat down.

I invited him in and motioned for him to continue.

"He's extremely depressed and angry. He has been inconsolable since the accident. He wants to be alone, and I don't know what to do." The man looked physically exhausted. Heavy bags hung under his eyes, telling the tale of many restless nights filled with prayer and worry, trying to help a struggling son who did not want saving. He, like many others, was looking for answers to alleviate the sting and lighten the burden of his child's trial. I'd often tell people in this situation that it's not the circumstances that determine our well being, but rather it's how we respond to them. It didn't even matter what the hardship was; if a patient chose to have a negative outlook on his or her condition, the outcome was always dire.

I wanted to help Jake, not just because it was my job but also because he was a fallen brother who shared my disability. After talking to Jake's dad, I reasoned that not only was Jake's body paralyzed but so too were his mind and his spirit.

"What's Jake's daily schedule?" I asked.

The father replied, "He doesn't have one." He continued, "He kicked his wife out. He wants nothing to do with our family. He's slowly going through and eliminating everyone from his life."

I looked at the father. "He is killing his social life before he kills himself."

The father's eyes filled with tears. "We know," he said. "He has no desire to deal with reality."

I nodded. "He thinks that by shutting himself out of reality, the truth will go away." I sighed sadly. "The longer he waits, the worse it will get. An accident like this does not get better. He's the only person who can change the situation."

As Jake's father continued to open up to me, I had already begun to formulate a game plan for a man with a mindset that at any given moment I could share. It was only a couple days later that I drove to Jake's house.

I knew that Jake came from a well-off family. Still, I was blown away when I pulled up to his home. It was not only massive and gorgeous but also completely handicap accessible. I noted the brand-new state-of-the-art wheelchair ramp outside. I noted how easy it was for me to get around and how nice it would be for anyone like me or Jake to have a home like that. I was even more surprised when I entered the home. I was let in by Jake's aide, who was just leaving and would return that evening. The house was empty except for her and Jake.

I called out my presence and heard a voice from somewhere in the home telling me to come in. As I wheeled through the house, I immediately noticed the absence of light, both physically and spiritually. There were no symbols of strength in the house either. No positive affirmations, no family pictures, no memories—it was void of anything that could lift one's spirits. A profound darkness hung in the air. Feeling more than a little uneasy, I called out once again for Jake. His voice called back to me, and I used it to guide myself to his room.

As I entered Jake's room, I saw that all the lights were off.

Having enough of the ominous feeling in the house, I didn't hesitate to flip on the lights.

This guy's whole life has been easy until now, I thought. *It's time to get uncomfortable.*

"Hey!" Jake cried out angrily. "Man! Turn off the lights!" His eyes squinted against the light, trying to adjust from the sudden brightness he was no longer accustomed to.

This is not going to go well, I thought.

"Jake, you're not used to the sun, brother," I responded. "I'm here to shed a bright light and eliminate the darkness you have put yourself in."

His eyes finally adjusting, Jake noticed my wheelchair for the first time and instantly recognized me. He smiled as he remembered me from our time together while he was a patient at the hospital.

Not stopping to think about what I was doing, I wheeled right over to Jake's bed. We looked at each other. In that moment, I had to fight hard to keep my emotions from taking over. Neither of us said a word, but like telepathy, both of us knew exactly how he felt. Seeing Jake in this situation and knowing just how close he was to leaving this world was almost consuming for me, and I thought my heart might break.

I dispensed with any formalities. We were way beyond any of that. After all, we held each other's thoughts and shared the same mind. We were part of club where no one wanted to be a member.

I watched as Jake pushed himself to a seated position. I spoke, scolding him like a mother would a child.

"Do you know what I would give to have what you have?!" Jake looked around.

"Not your money," I said, rolling my eyes. "Your upper-body strength! You have your arms!" I almost shouted. "Don't you realize? This could be so much worse."

I could see the array of prescription drugs on Jake's nightstand and immediately knew he was self-medicating. He, like me, suffered from horrific nerve pain. Unlike me, he used meds to dull the pain. Long ago, I had chosen a sound mind with almost constant pain, in lieu of dulled discomfort and absent thoughts. From the sheer amount of meds he was taking, I knew that he was well over his allotted limit.

"Jake, you're surviving life, but you're not living," I said sadly. "Life will not bring you the happiness you desire until you decide to find it."

It was clear that he had been doing nothing since returning home from the hospital. He had no desire left to fight for his life and reclaim his peace and happiness. Determined to help Jake turn his life around, I started out by making him his own personal mission statement. On a piece of paper I wrote, "Stand Up, Until It Stands Down."

I left it at the foot of his bed. There he could look at it each day and hopefully get the courage to come back.

Before I had come, I had developed a game plan, but now that I was here and after talking briefly to Jake, I could see that the situation was far worse than I had realized. This young man had everything money could buy: a large and beautiful home brimming with lavish furniture and accessories that would make anyone feel like a star. He also had a woman who loved him, a caring family, toys, cars, and even a job, if he desired it. Yet here he was, all alone and refusing to let anyone in.

When I realized nothing I could say would force Jake to come back, I simply asked if I could pray. He had once been spiritual but had let it slip away. There were so many red flags that inside I knew it would be a miracle for Jake to stay and fight. Still I prayed for that miracle. I wanted him to see this had nothing to do with my job and everything to do with me genuinely caring about him. I prayed for there to be good spirit in his home, as it was so desperately needed.

After our visit, I called Jake's counselor and told him it was bad. "There is no light in him or the house," I said. "Jake has to be accountable. He has to have small goals." I knew it would be a long road for Jake if he chose to return, but I wanted to fight for him, and I was willing to wait.

Jake and I continued to work together for many weeks. Unfortunately, no matter what I said or how hard I tried to bring light into his life, he chose darkness instead. It was as if the devil himself had control over all of Jake's actions. It seems that he targets those of us who are going through adversity the hardest. Using his influence, he chases God's lambs far from the herd and protection of our loving Heavenly Father, Savior, family, and friends. His goal is to isolate us, to make us feel like we're weak and not good enough or strong enough to live a happy and healthy life. If we choose to stay away, if we chose to feed these negative influences, if we stay there, we will not recover.

As weeks turned into months, I sat frustrated and helpless at Jake's utter lack of desire to help his situation get better. One day as I left his house, I thought of a pine tree that used to sit outside my childhood home. The tree was as big as it was beautiful. The perfect addition to our neighborhood, it stood impressively near our front yard, showing off its many needles and huge branches. I loved it and admired it. It had been there long before we had bought that home. I climbed it often, sat in its strong branches, and thought it to be the biggest, toughest tree in the whole world. One night, there was a massive windstorm. I watched dumbfounded as a strong gust of wind came and pushed the pine tree to the ground. It had been with me for years, yet one wind gust had blown it over. I could not believe or understand how that could happen. A closer look at my tree would reveal that it was hollow. Though it looked majestic on the outside, it had nothing to sustain it on the inside.

On my last visit with Jake, I knew that because nothing was changing, I would not be able to come anymore. I was heartbroken and more than a little frustrated. Here Jake had everything, yet he had nothing. In that moment it was clear to me why a loving Father in Heaven allows us and encourages us to do hard things. We will need the strength those moments provide when the storm comes. Like my tree, on the outside Jake seemed majestic—certainly his life looked beautiful—but inside, the substance that could have saved him, like my hollow pine tree, was simply not there. He had let it go.

Larry Y. Wilson once said, "The arrival of a typhoon is no time to dust off the gift of the Holy Ghost and figure out how to use it. . . . We need the Holy Spirit as our guide in calm waters so His voice will be unmistakable to us in the fiercest storm."[12]

God had not stopped speaking to Jake. Jake had stopped listening.

My heart was more than a little heavy as I left Jake on my last day working with him. I did not blame Jake—and how could I? I had been there before and at any given moment could be right there again. It simply hurt that I could not force Jake to see that he was worth saving, wheelchair and all.

On my way back home, I called and recommended that Jake not be left alone, stating that he needed twenty-four-hour supervision.

A few months later, Jake took his life.

Jake's choice to leave this world was a warning for me to make sure that I stay in control of my environment and my circumstances. Truthfully it scared me. I knew that I could never be complacent. Rolling into Jake's home with no lights on that first day, I could feel the devil was at the door and had full control of the environment. It's interesting the two choices we can make with adversity. The Lord wants us to use our adversities to become truly great in the world by overcoming them. The devil wants us to become so discouraged by our adversities that we totally give up and let them overcome us.

Though I believe that Jake has found peace, and I am grateful for that, and though there have been times I have even envied him, I genuinely think that someone upstairs is keeping track of all my efforts to stay here and live a life worthy of returning to God. One day I hope to cash in on that.

Choosing to fight daily battles is no easy task. It is so easy to be negative and takes far more work to be positive. Only

---

12. "Take the Holy Spirit as Your Guide," *Ensign*, May 2018.

when I don't give into the anger, when I choose to embrace my weaknesses, am I able to see another side of this disability. In the beginning, like the man I had seen die in the ICU and Jake, I refused to even think there was another side. Surely the only things that could come out of both my disabilities were anger, frustration, sadness, and despair. Yet once I acknowledged what the anger was doing to me, I knew I couldn't keep it going. So I did the impossible. I let it go.

Instead of reaching down in anger, sadness, and selfishness, I began to try and reach up in positivity, offering my soul and heart to my Savior to help see me through. Something beautiful began to happen after that: instead of worrying all the time, I became hopeful. The only thing that changed to make my difficulties a little more tolerable was me.

A change of heart coupled with the Lord's grace little by little helped me see all weaknesses as great potentials for strength, not only for me but also for those around me. We all have inherent weaknesses, either by our own design or from personal and unique adversities. Our greatest victories and disappointments in life come through them. They can make us bitter, or they can make us better. I so admire those who allow their negative circumstances to dictate positive outcomes. Though I had patients who chose to end their journey, I had far more who chose to begin it. Those were the stories that filled me with hope in my own journey and helped shape me into who I am.

Chapter 18

CHOOSING TO CLIMB

One of my favorite patients was Robert Hales, a great man of faith. Overcoming debilitating nerve damage in his legs stemming from a blood clot, he had been staying at the neuro-rehab facility for the past four weeks. As it just so happened, I too had the same incapacitating pain and understood all too well what this great man was going through. It was my pleasure to be able to work with him. Each time I rolled into his room, I'd put on a big smile and say, "How's my favorite patient today?" before I'd provide him a review of what his doctor and therapist were working on.

My favorite part of working with this beloved patient was learning from him and his love for his Father in Heaven. In return, it was my job to teach him how to deal with physically and mentally incapacitating nerve pain.

"You know, they say the purpose in mortality is to gain a body and to be tested," he told me one day. "But it's also to be tested *in* your body." He paused. "There are twenty-eight rooms here with people going through their own trials of their bodies.

We must all be tested in all things." He finished humbly, "I'm no different than they are."

The day Robert Hales was discharged, I rolled into his room one last time.

"I guess they're kicking you out," I joked. "As hard as I tried to keep you here, they just wouldn't listen." I grinned. "They said you're making such great progress that you're ready to go home."

He looked at me, smiling kindly. I watched as tears filled his eyes.

"Brandon, I don't know how you do it," he said. "Dealing with nerve pain and all of your physical limitations. The nerve pain that I have experienced in my leg is by far and above the worst physical pain I have ever dealt with."

As I heard this man of God humbly and compassionately speak to me, tears instantly filled my own eyes. "It is bearable," I replied, "because of my faith. Knowing that one day I will eventually rest from it."

He spoke once again. "I'm amazed that you have come so far living with this pain for the past eleven years. You are such a great example to me and to many others on this floor."

My heart filled with gratitude for this great man and for the opportunity I'd had to work with him. As tears rolled down my cheeks, I spoke again. "You know, you haven't been the easiest patient to see. What do I possibly say to encourage someone as good as you that you don't already know?"

He smiled at me once more and said, "Brandon, I know that you speak from experience and I know that you live your life pushing forward. The best words I've heard on this rehab unit are the words you say each time you roll into my room, 'Push, brother, push.'"

One morning, I received a new patient, a cute girl named Jessica who was only a junior in high school. A couple of months before we met, Jessica had received the same devastating diagnosis I had received at her age: paralysis, hers from the waist down. She had been riding shotgun in an ATV with a boy who had asked her out on a date, and then the ATV rolled, pinning Jessica and breaking her neck.

As I wheeled toward Jessica, I was very aware that while seeing me could be a sense of great comfort for her, it could also be extremely devastating. I knew she planned to walk again, just as I did and still do, and seeing me might solidify any comments from doctors or family about her never achieving that goal, since here I was eleven years later still in a chair.

After introducing myself to Jessica, I told her to follow me, to push where I pushed. It took us a while to get to the elevators. With every exhausting push, Jessica was learning firsthand just how difficult this new journey would be. As I waited for her to catch up, I remembered how hard it was in the beginning to push even just a few feet.

While Jessica sat at the bottom of a huge mountain, just beginning her climb, through her I could see how far I had really come over the past decade.

I knew where I wanted to take her.

IMC is nestled in the middle of the Salt Lake Valley, with the rehab floor twelve stories up. Jokingly I often told my patients, "You better learn to get out of bed, because if there's a fire, you and I will be parachuting off this building together."

Once Jessica had finally gotten inside the elevator, I pushed the button that would take us to the top floor. The doors closed, opening again to a beautiful sight. Once again, I told Jessica to follow me as I led us to the huge windows that overlooked the lofty and magnificent Wasatch Front mountains. Rising out of the Salt Lake Valley floor, they tower over ten thousand feet in the air.

We parked our wheelchairs side by side.

Pointing out the window, I asked her, "What do you see elevating high above the Salt Lake Valley skyline?" It was the same question I asked every patient beginning his or her journey.

"I see mountains," Jessica replied.

I nodded. "Yes, but describe them to me in detail."

She paused. "Some parts are really pretty. Some are ugly. There are lots of jagged rocks and some smoother places. They're massive too."

When she was done, I spoke. "What are the challenges you're currently facing in your life that you would like to conquer?"

For many patients, it was to regain a sense of control from lost capacities physically, mentally, or emotionally after accidents or injuries. For those like Jessica and me, it's always the same answer.

"I want to walk again," she responded.

I could hear myself saying those same words years ago as she said them out loud to me. I remembered clearly every well-meaning person who had entered my hospital room those three months after my spinal cord injury. Every single one of them told me that they knew I would walk again. Often this was accompanied with the same phrase: "You just need to have faith." What they didn't understand was that no one had more faith or hope or said more prayers than me. No one wanted it more than I did. I knew everyone loved me and was devastated with all I was going through, but their words, though meant to be encouraging, became overwhelming to me.

A common misconception we have, perhaps more so as Christians, is that faith is the cure-all. Sometimes we get stuck in our thinking that *A* plus *B* equals *C*. If we pray enough, are good people, keep the commandments, or whatever else, then we will be protected from loss and heartache, and more important, we will be entitled to miracles.

Though it is true that faith can and does cause miracles (I have witnessed this in my own life), faith always has to be combined with God's will for us. All the faith in the world was not going to make Jessica or me walk again if that wasn't God's plan for us. In the same way that being paralyzed or any other tragedies we all suffer aren't punishments for lack of faith. Life is unpredictable. Life will happen to all of us, regardless of who we are or what we believe. Faith may not change unwanted outcomes, but it *is* the incredible power that can help us get through them.

I looked at Jessica. "Jessica," I said, "I am not your future."

Her brow furrowed.

"Don't you ever look at me and think your fate is the same as mine," I told her. "Whether you walk again is up to you and especially God. There isn't a day that goes by that I don't hope I will walk again, but so far that has not been God's plan for me," I said. "However, just because I am not walking doesn't mean you won't. God's plan for you is different than His plan for me. Don't you dare ever give up that hope, just as I don't."

Jessica's eyes filled with tears as we then spoke of faith and miracles. "Perhaps what is more powerful than faith is trust," I told her. "Trust in the Almighty's plan for both of us. Trust that there is a purpose for allowing us, irrespective of our immense faith, to sit in excruciating moments far longer than we'd ever want." I paused. "Sadly, people make one of the biggest mistakes you can make during periods of great trials. They turn from

God in the very time they need Him the most." I continued, "No situation has ever become easier because one has turned from God. Distancing oneself from light and hope leaves only darkness with no way to see how to navigate new and difficult paths. In contrast, if we let His light shine, we can see that this path is not a dead end. Though different than what we'd pick, it too has a journey worth taking."

I pled with Jessica to stay strong, to continue pushing alongside me each day. One of the hardest things to witness along with debilitating fear was a patient who stopped pushing forward when adjusting to recent challenges in life. I witnessed it happen countless times. Instead of fighting, they sat and waited. They waited, and they hoped. They even prayed that things would get better while they sat. However, there was no visible sign of action or real intent on their part to make their situation better. The longer they waited, the worse it got. It was devastating to see how many people chose that path.

"Faith without works is dead" (James 2:17). When we add faith and trust together, our trials can then equal hope, patience, love, greater understanding, help to our fellow man, and a closer relationship with our Father in Heaven as we lean on Him more than we ever have before. Faith and trust are even more powerful when combined with hard work.

It was inspiring to watch those who chose to work and to fight, those who were willing to do all in their power to make their situation better. Jessica became one of those people.

Pointing once again to the mountain that Jessica had just described, I said, "See that big, beautiful mountain? That is your mountain, Jessica." I turned to her. "There will be scary parts, ugly and beautiful parts, rough terrain and smooth terrain. You will fall again and again. Sometimes you will fall so far that you will almost be back to where you started." Placing my hands on hers, I finished, "You must climb your mountain alone. Nobody can make you climb it but you."

Jessica and I embraced after that. We cried for some time by that big window, staring at the obstacle I was still climbing and the one she had just arrived at looming in the distance. After a few moments, I looked at Jessica again. "I'm still not done climbing that mountain, and honestly, I don't know when I will make it to the top, but my family has been there every step of the way, cheering me on, just as I know yours will be there for you." I smiled at her. "Our paths are on the same mountain. They are right next to each other. I'll be climbing right there beside you." A slew of images filled my mind of my own climb and how my view had changed over the years.

I left Jessica that day with the same scripture I left all my new patients, regardless of whether they believed in God. Many of them posted it right next to the TV in their room so that it was always looking back at them during their stay.

"Thou hast enlarged my steps under me, that my feet did not slip. . . . When I said, My foot slippeth; thy mercy, O Lord, held me up" (Psalms 18:36; 94:18).

Every patient that was discharged on our floor did a victory lap around the twelfth-floor hallways while a song of their choosing blasted through the speakers overhead. A fanfare of doctors and therapists and I cheered and then warmly embraced each of them as they continued their climb outside the hospital, toward their goals, or as they accepted their reality that they would leave this life earlier than they had wanted.

For those of you waiting to conquer your challenges, what are you waiting for? Now is the time in mortality to start climbing mountains. Some mountains we may never see the top of in this life. However, our view is always better the higher we climb.

The day after my spinal injury, I was told of a new drug that could possibly give me some movement back, making it so that I wasn't completely quadriplegic. The drug, however, was not approved for use in Utah because it was still in the trial stages. Worse still, there was only a forty-eight-hour window in which the drug was effective. My family and I were desperate to be given permission to use it. We appealed to Utah's senator at the time to approve the drug. He immediately went to work. At forty-two hours after my accident, the drug was approved and given to me. Consequently, I was given back some movement in my upper body and, therefore, independence.

Eleven years later, I would have the privilege of counseling and working with this same senator's granddaughter, Jessica, after her own paralyzing accident. There are no coincidences in this life.

After she was discharged, Jessica returned weekly to show me the progress she had made. One day, when she returned, she walked through the doors with the assistance of a cane. How grateful I am that Jessica did not give up and instead chose to climb.

I do not know when the Lord will see fit to allow me the privilege of walking again, but until then, I, like Jessica, will continue to climb. I bet the view from the top is pretty amazing, and I don't want to miss it.

Chapter 19

DIRTY PLACES, SICKLY OUTCOMES, AND ANOTHER CLOSED DOOR

Pushing myself with my hands leaves me in contact with whatever my wheels roll over, making me more susceptible than the average person to the many pathogens that inhabit hospitals. As each year passed with me working at IMC, I got weaker and sicker. After only four years at my job, it became evident that my quadriplegic body couldn't keep up with my drive.

Because it took so long to get me ready in the mornings, my home health aide would have to show up at 5:00 a.m. to get me to work by 9:30. The four hours it took to get me out the door each day—coupled with the lack of sleep each night, due to my nerve pain—absolutely exhausted me by the time I even got to my car. I didn't return home until 7:00 in the evenings. All day, I pushed my paralyzed body to fulfill the workload of an able-bodied person.

The most common hospital-acquired infection is a urinary tract infection. Since I had to catheterize myself in the hospital bathrooms throughout the day, it made my risk of getting a UTI greater. The nurses who worked with me and cared about me as if I were one of their patients often commented that I wasn't looking well. They were usually right too. No matter how hard I tried to keep my hands clean, I was getting sick all the time at the hospital. My doctors prescribed me antibiotics to treat my infections, but little by little the bacteria became more resistant to the various medications as the frequency at which I received UTIs increased.

One of the doctors I worked with on the rehab unit noticed that each time I developed a UTI I would lose much of my energy, causing muscle spasms throughout my body. At times my legs would shake so uncontrollably that they'd physically bounce out of my wheelchair. As the UTIs became worse and the antibiotics became less effective, the danger went from annoying to potentially fatal as I learned that I could go septic and die from these constant contaminants. Many nights, I arrived home totally dejected.

"I don't know how much longer I can do this," I told my mom one evening. "My body is breaking down. My job is literally killing me."

While my parents' biggest concern was that I would eventually die from the constant UTIs, I felt forgotten by the Lord. He'd blessed me with the ability to graduate from college and had directed me toward this job, and now I wondered why. Could it possibly be that He only wanted me to work for four years after going to school for eight? Would He really do that to me after all I had already been through? Was my life not hard enough? Here I was trying to be a role model and give hope to people in the same situations as me, and it was working. I was *actually* making a difference. I was thrilled to genuinely be of use in an able-bodied world. I could not comprehend why God would take from me the one good thing I was able to do. Why save me from all my other accidents? Why keep me here on earth only to let me die from a hospital infection after working such a short period of time? Surely God's purpose for me was not to live alone at home doing nothing. It all felt so pointless, so cruel.

Under the effects of all I was going through and pushing myself to do, I was crumbling physically. However, I reasoned that at least I was independent. At least I was working. At least I was making a difference. At least I had a life that mattered. So I continued to push, knowing what the outcome would likely be but refusing to face it. At the same time I was fighting sickness, I watched the parallels between my life and that of my patients. Many were suffering the same effects of getting sick and weak like I was, but in a different way.

While I pushed through dirty places in the hospital that physically made me ill, some of my patients lived their lives amongst destructive habits and attitudes that eventually infected their bodies and souls. Those who chose to live a life amongst dirty things could not escape the eventual outcome of getting dirty. The side effects of their choices ultimately led them to the hospital with suicidal attempts or drug overdoses. While the doctors treated their symptoms, I tried to stop the cause behind them.

It's amazing how resistant our ability to overcome bad decisions can be if left unchecked. Scientific evidence suggests that it takes approximately ninety days for the brain to reset itself and shake off the influence of an existing bad habit.[13] And

---

13. Michael D. Lemonick, "How We Get Addicted," *Time*, July 2007.

shake them off we must, if we want to move forward and stop getting sick. We cannot expect to live healthy and happy lives pushing through dirty places. Sometimes it's unnoticeable. We may not feel the effects right off—maybe a dose of antibiotic keeps it at bay for a bit—but with time these choices to live lower than our potential affect us like bad bacteria, leading us toward sickly outcomes. If not noticed and treated quickly, they can ultimately kill us, spiritually, mentally, and physically.

I did what I could, teaching my patients how to use antibiotics of the soul to treat and prevent these infections. Once I identified what pollutants were responsible for their illnesses, I formulated an individual plan of action to treat them. Often it was necessary to discharge them to drug treatment programs and safe houses. There they could recover in clean environments, begin the process of rebuilding their lives, and begin to establish positive habits.

There were far too many patients who had developed such a negative view of life and of themselves that recovery was almost impossible. In the short time I had amongst them, I tried my best to make them understand that they were far more than what they saw in the mirror. Sadly, I was not always successful. When that happened, it was extremely difficult on me. However, it was during those times that I realized for the first time in many years that I was not the one who was handicapped.

Although I continued to push forward and help my patients despite what felt like never-ending illness, during my fifth year of work there came a point when I knew something needed to change. I prayed that I would be directed to what I should do. Nothing came to me except more UTIs. I couldn't quit my job, not after all the hard work and the many years of schooling it took to get here. Quitting wasn't in my vocabulary either, and

I was too mad about my situation to even think about resigning. I had to be independent. It gave me the confidence and the self-esteem needed to live the life I had been called to live. As an added bonus, I could financially support myself, which was a wonderful feeling of achievement.

As scared as I was and as much as I didn't want to face it, I knew that something had to change. Life, once again, was not meant to go by my design but by His. By now, after all the accidents I had been through and how many times God had chosen to keep me here, I knew working myself to death was not an option, nor was it my call to make. Something had to change. Waiting for an answer to my prayers, I kept pressing forward. As is often the case in this unpredictable world and certainly in my life, that answer came in a way that I didn't expect or want.

Tuesday, December 3, 2013, started like most mornings. My home health aide arrived at 5:45 a.m. that day. A cold front had just moved in the night before, bringing with it snow that began to fall around 11:30 p.m. I knew the snowy conditions would make driving a bit more challenging and was hoping it would let up before I left for work. Thankfully, it stopped snowing around 8:00 a.m.

After I was dressed and ready for the day, I went upstairs to find my mom waiting to help get me breakfast. She had the TV turned to the news and commented that she didn't want me driving in these conditions. As we were eating, we heard many reports of accidents and cars that had slid off the roads.

"I wish you didn't have to go to work this morning," my mom repeated.

My mom has remarked that after the first couple of accidents I'd gone through, she actually worried about me less. She understood that the Lord obviously had a purpose for me still being on the earth. If He hadn't taken me those other times when I truly should have died, then when He finally did, she would know it was because it was my time to go and part of God's plan. If it wasn't so, then why bring me back all the other times? She relies immensely on the Spirit and knows it will let her know if I am in danger, and if it does not, then it is time for me to go. It may sound strange, but that thought brings her peace. It brings me peace too. Both of us know we are not in control here.

Even though there is peace and faith, my mom has always been very cautious with me, and certainly no one can blame her. So I regarded her warnings that morning as her being overly worried. Though I was also aware of the frequency at which accidents seemed to happen to me, at the same time, I had to live my life. That meant getting up early in the morning and going to work, just like any other person would, regardless of weather conditions. To be honest, it felt good, like I was showing my disability who's boss.

After reassuring my mom that I would be just fine, I got in my truck and left for work. It looked like conditions had improved dramatically. Just to be safe, however, I put my Ford F-150 into four-wheel drive to give me more grip on the roads.

I had driven paralyzed for the past sixteen years at that point and had put over one hundred thousand miles on my truck. I have never been pulled over for speeding, nor had I ever come close to being in a car accident. I consider myself to be a very safe driver. However, just before that day, I'd had several dreams in which I was driving in my truck and was suddenly unable to stop. In these dreams, I'd try to slam down my hand brake, but it wouldn't work fast enough to stop my truck in time. The dreams always ended with me crashing into a couple of cars. Because the dreams were so vivid, they had a carryover effect of me being extra cautious. Each time I left the house, I would check my hand controls often and make sure everything was working properly.

With memories of those dreams fresh in my mind, combined with my mom's worries that morning, I made a point to drive more carefully and slower than usual, even though the roads were pretty much clear by that time. Not too long after I had gotten on the freeway, traffic started to slow down. Emergency lights flashed in the distance. There appeared to be a car accident up ahead. I was in the left lane, which is where I generally choose to drive because my reaction time to stop is a little slower than the average driver, because I use hand controls. I also prefer to be next to the emergency lane, where I can pull over or move around problem traffic if needed.

As I drew closer to the accident, I started to slow from roughly sixty miles an hour to fifty. I saw the HOV lane on my left was blocked by emergency crews attending to the minor car accident. Suddenly, out of the corner of my eye, a small sedan abruptly darted past me from the far-right lane. To my astonishment, the woman driving aggressively cut across all three lanes of traffic and attempted a U-turn to try to get into the blocked HOV lane. Unbeknownst to me at the time, the woman's husband was involved in the accident that the emergency crew was attending to. In her state of panic, she had driven erratically and was now facing north on the southbound highway and directly in my lane. I had little to no reaction time.

Instantly I knew I had no place to turn to safely avoid a collision. Either I swerved left and hit the emergency vehicles or I swerved right and hit the cars traveling next to me. The only other option was to stay in my lane and hit the woman head on.

Some people say time slows when you go through these types of accidents. For me, it did not. It happened quickly and violently. The oncoming car angrily struck the front of my truck. The impact was physically unforgiving and brutal. Intense, sharp pain from the clock peg on my steering wheel and from the air bag smashing my face hit me all at once. As if I had received a knockout punch to the head, I reeled for a moment, dazed at what had just happened. I found it difficult to keep my head up and noticed my vision had gone blurry. Through my cracked windshield, I could just make out the hood of my truck. Peeled back like it had been opened by a can opener, it blocked part of my vision. I wondered how I had survived. That thought quickly turned to panic, however, as my truck continued to roll down the highway and headed straight for a parked tow truck. If the first impact hadn't killed me, I was sure this one would finish me off. Physically and mentally powerless after the initial hit, I watched helplessly as my truck headed for another.

As I grimaced and waited for impact, I thought how odd it was to have cheated death three times only to die like this. I was strangely at peace knowing there was nothing I could do about it. Squeezing my eyes shut, I hit the corner of the back end of the tow truck hard. This accident, although at a slower speed, was far worse. Not only could I see it coming, but also the damage after the hit was costlier since my air bag had already deployed and now there was nothing to protect my head.

Once again, I felt the impact propel my body forward. As my face came in contact with what must have been the steering wheel, blood immediately began to pour from my nose. When I was able to look up, I was horrified to see that the corner of the tow truck had crashed through my windshield, stopping just inches from my face. When I turned to my rearview mirror to assess the damage, it was obvious my nose was broken severely in several locations. I groaned out loud as the pain consumed me.

Frantically, I grabbed my phone hanging in its usual spot around my neck. Trying to call my mom, each time I attempted to dial, blood from my nose pooled on my cell phone, making it too difficult to find the right numbers to push. Desperate to talk to her, I thought I had a very real chance of dying—and quickly. After having already gone through a major traumatic brain injury in my youth, I knew how dangerous another hard blow to my head could be, and I had just experienced two consecutively. It was the one thing my neurosurgeons had constantly reminded me of back then, after a six-hour-long brain surgery to relieve my subdural hematoma: *do not hit your head*. During that surgery, they placed non-visible screws in my head that were used to strengthen my skull and protect the weak area where the brunt of the impact took place. I knew immediately that I had just been hit hard enough for there to be potential life-threatening bleeding in my brain. I had to tell my mom I loved her in case I lost consciousness and would never respond again.

After trying to wave down the highway patrol officers and paramedics who were only ten yards away from me, attending to the other accident, I saw a couple of highway patrol officers running toward my vehicle. I thought how fortunate I was to be alive—not only that, but how grateful I was that the accident had happened where it had. Only a matter of yards separated me from hitting the emergency personnel.

When I was finally able to punch the right numbers on my phone, my mom answered the call. I told her what had happened. She immediately asked if I was okay. Quickly assuring her that I was, I placed the phone on speaker so that I could communicate with the highway patrol and she could hear the conversation. Leaving the phone on speaker mode gave both of us peace that we were connected through this ordeal.

A couple of the officers got to my car.

"Are you all right?" one officer asked me.

"I think so," I said. "But it looks like my nose is busted up pretty bad."

"Yeah," he said, nodding. "We can see that. Try not to touch it."

The other officer interrupted, "Are you hurt anywhere else? Can you move your legs?"

The accident happened so quickly that the officers didn't notice my mangled wheelchair in the back of my truck. They had no idea I was paralyzed.

"No, I can't move my legs at all. I'm paralyzed from the neck on down," I told them. "I'll need some help to pull me out."

As they glanced at each other with looks of panic and fear on their faces, I understood that they thought my injuries were much more severe than they could see. They must have thought it was amazing that I was able to not only diagnose that I was paralyzed (and from the neck on down, no less) but also be so calm about it.

Although I was dazed, I quickly reassured them. "No, no. I'm already paralyzed from the neck on down."

That only seemed to confuse them more. I'm sure they were thinking, *How are you driving?!*

In a lot of pain, I cut to the chase. "I've been paralyzed for many years from a previous accident and am a quadriplegic. I'm going to need your help because I can't open my door and my captain's chair is busted."

Although still puzzled by how I was able to drive, they quickly motioned for several other paramedics to assist me. The paramedics cut me out of my seatbelt and securely transferred me to their gurney. I could tell everyone was very surprised that I was so calm.

I finally said, "Guys, this isn't my first rodeo." I paused. "In fact, I have frequent flier miles on Life Flight."

They didn't know what I meant, and I didn't bother to explain.

I looked at a paramedic. "You saw the accident, right?" I asked him.

"Yes, I did," he responded. "You're fortunate to be alive. That lady just about pulled a widow maker on you."

"Is she okay?" I asked.

"Yes, by some miracle," he replied.

When he said that, I was a little bit more relaxed. Not because I felt lucky to be alive but because I feared that the car insurance company would claim that because of my physical disability, I had put others and myself at greater risk while driving. If that had been the case, I could have lost my license.

"Please write in your report that there was no way for me to avoid that accident," I asked the officer.

The officer saw my look of concern and said, "Don't worry. We all saw what you saw. In fact, we're grateful you didn't swerve. If you had, it could have killed us."

As they loaded me in the ambulance, I turned my neck as much as I was able so that I could look at my truck. I knew it was totaled and this was likely the last time I would ever see it again. That was a tough day. It wasn't just a car to me. It was my freedom, and I had just lost it. I wasn't just saying good-bye to a loved one. I was saying good-bye to driving in the mountains, to dating, to hanging out with friends and family, and now to work. The last thought took my breath away. . . . work. *How am I going to keep my job?* Even as I thought it, I knew the answer.

My dilemma of how I was going to continue working at the hospital while constantly getting sick had just been decided for me.

Chapter 20

BROKEN THINGS

The drive from the ambulance to the hospital went quickly, but my breathing was giving me fits. By this time, my nose had swollen significantly and the dried blood inside it was blocking off a lot of the airflow. Consequently, the blood that was still running went toward the path of least resistance: down my throat. Unable to use my diaphragm or stomach muscles, with the assistance of the paramedics, I began to cough up the blood so I wouldn't suffocate. It reminded me of every classic movie I've ever seen where it shows a character coughing up blood just before dying. Concerned, I asked one of the paramedics, "The blood I'm coughing up is coming from my nose, right?"

"We believe so," one responded.

That's not reassuring or comforting, I thought, still very concerned the blood was coming from my brain.

My family arrived at the ER shortly after I did. After assuring them that I was okay, a doctor let us know that because of all the metal in my body from previous injuries and the nature and intensity of the crash, they'd be taking me in for an MRI/CT scan to make sure there wasn't anything else going on.

After I got back from having the scans taken, my family and I waited in my room anxiously. All of us wondered if this would finally be the accident that took me. If not, if I stayed, would I be the same? And always in the back of our minds: if I was meant to be here, then why did these events keep happening?

We already knew I would have to undergo extensive facial surgeries to fix my broken nose, but we weren't yet sure if there was anything else wrong. My mom held up a portable mirror for me to look at myself. To be honest, I was nervous to look. The last time I had looked in the mirror, there was a handsome man staring back at me. I was hoping he was still there. With some hesitation, my eyes slowly moved up to the mirror until they found the stranger peering back at me. It felt like I was looking through a distorted mirror at a theme park.

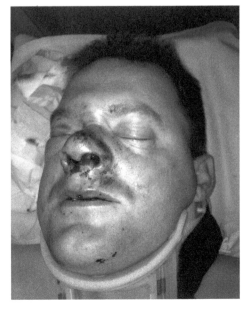

Left this morning looking like beauty, and showed up to the hospital as beast, I jokingly thought. My face was swollen to the size of a melon, and I could barely see through my eyelids, which refused to open. I sighed. "I've seen enough. . . . thanks," I told my mom. I was now confident it wasn't just my nose that was broken.

As more and more time passed, I became increasingly concerned about the fact that the doctors still hadn't returned to my room. I started to get so anxious that I had to try and settle myself down. I knew all too well that the longer I waited, the worse the news would be.

When the doctor finally came to see me, he let us know that I had multiple facial and orbital fractures, as well as numerous fractures in my nose. He then told me that the scans revealed that I had some cerebral spinal fluid swelling in my skull, a result of my nose being jammed violently upward by my steering column. He mentioned that he believed they could fix the nose and other fractures with facial surgery, but they wanted to keep me in the hospital for a few days to monitor the cerebral spinal fluid swelling.

"Thanks, but I'd rather just work at this hospital than become a patient," I told the doctor.

He nodded sympathetically before telling me I had to stay.

"Then at least clock me in, so I get paid," I joked half-heartedly.

I kept thinking, *How is it that I can work at this hospital for five years yet still know more about being a patient here than being an employee?*

I heard the doctor mention that they wouldn't be able to start my facial reconstruction surgeries until the swelling in my face went down, adding that it would likely be ten to fifteen days away. He proceeded to let me know that they were going to have to remove shattered segments of my right orbital bone and replace them with a titanium plate to keep my eyes from sinking inside my eye sockets. He mentioned that once I was discharged in a couple of days, I could return home, but I would need to come back for outpatient surgery in two weeks. Exhausted from the accident and all the meds they had given me and trying to process what my life would look like after all of this, I was on the verge of shutting down.

Seeing this, my doctor looked at me sympathetically, not wanting to be the bearer of one more piece of bad news. He momentarily hesitated before speaking again. "We believe the swelling in your nose is keeping the cerebral spinal fluid from draining out. However, once the swelling goes down, it may become clear to us that it is in fact leaking."

My dad cut the doctor off, asking the question none of us wanted an answer to: "What happens if it's leaking?"

I held my breath.

The doctor paused. "There's a high likelihood that your son will need to have brain surgery," he said.

My heart sunk.

I knew what brain surgery entailed. The staples. The hundreds of stiches. The migraines and mood swings. The sympathetic and unsympathetic blatant stares. The fears of falling and hitting my head. Another huge scar. The mental rehab. The stuttering . . . The restarting.

While my doctor had the degree, I felt like the expert. I knew all the terminology, the body language, the subtle way their eyes shifted when they talked to me on a need-to-know basis and then took my parents out in the hall and delivered another harsh dose of reality to two people already dealing with the harshest. In that moment, as the doctor spoke and my parents and siblings absorbed his words, I saw a new trial. Though I had thought I was carrying all I could carry, I would be required to take on more. Even as that thought hit me, I knew that I could not. This was my rock bottom.

As the doctor spoke, my mind swallowed me up, saving me from a sorrow too big to carry for an entire family, let alone one man. Heartache was already my constant companion. I knew it intimately. At times it expanded so vastly that it not only filled my soul but also reached out and touched those who were closest to me, giving them a glimpse of the grief that is so much a part of me, it *is* me. Other times it was almost merciful as it lifted slightly and momentarily allowed me to breathe before quickly returning home.

I closed my eyes and allowed myself to slip away. A familiar melody began to play inside my mind. I could hear my favorite artist, Sting, singing "Why Should I Cry for You?" It was one of my favorite songs that he has written. Sting's dad had wanted him to go to sea one day. He never did get that chance. However, he wrote his father this song about what might have happened had he gone.

Sting's quiet, melodic voice sang to me, willing my troubled mind to listen to his words, "Asleep on the ocean's bed, drifting on empty seas. For all my days remaining."[14]

Tears clung to the corners of my eyes as I let the words speak my heaviness. How long I had been drifting.

"But would north be true? Why should I? Why should I cry for you?"[15]

As the lyrics played in my mind, I spoke to my Heavenly Father. *Why? Why am I am always having to cry for You?*

Why am I still here? The more I drift, the emptier I get. Am I heading true north? Am I even heading east or west or south?

If You want me here so bad, then why all of these major accidents? Why not leave me alone and just let me be here? Why can't there be some hardships I can overcome on my own, like so many other people in this world? Why must it be necessary for me to continuously have to turn to You because my burdens are too heavy to carry alone? Am I even heading the right way? What is Your path for me?

---

14. Track 5 on *The Soul Cages*, A&M, 1991.
15. Sting, "Why Should I Cry for You?"

I knew what the next line of the song would say before I heard Sting's voice sing it to me. I had repeated it so many times, over so many years. "Dark angels follow me over a godless sea," Sting sang in my mind. "Mountains of endless falling. For all my days remaining."[16]

That was all my life was going to be until I died: dark angels following me, mountains of endless falling, for all my days remaining.

This was too much. This was the end. There were already too many holes to plug in my sinking vessel, yet another giant one had just opened up.

How, Father? How can I face another challenge of this magnitude? I've already had brain surgery. Will You require that I have it again while paralyzed with an already fragile brain? How? Why? Have I done something wrong?

Sting continued to sing my lamentations. "Sometimes I see your face. . . . Why must I think of you?"[17]

Sometimes, I feel so close to You that it's almost as if I can see You. How can You feel such immense love for me yet allow me to suffer so greatly? My faith could move a mountain, but You hold it in place. Why? Have I not done enough? Is my fight not already too much?

This will sink me.

As I asked the questions over and over, Sting sang in the back of my mind, "Why must I? Why should I? Why should I cry for you? Why would you want me to?"[18]

God, why must I do it over and over again? Before sleep mercifully took over, I asked one last question: *If You love me, why would You want me to?*

---

16. "Why Should I Cry for You?"
17. "Why Should I Cry for You?"
18. "Why Should I Cry for You?"

That night I asked my little sister Bridgett to stay and sleep in my room. I spent that entire night pleading with my Heavenly Father to calm my raging seas and spare me from the approaching storm.

For two days, I did not stop pleading with God to heal my broken facial bones and to stop any cerebral fluid from leaking, sparing me from brain surgery. More important, I asked my Father in Heaven to heal my wounded soul—that if it was not part of His plan to take away this trial, then somehow He would bless me with strength beyond what I already had, what I was already giving, so that I could endure what was to come. I knew what was in me would not be enough. It was already being used to carry me through each day.

So I prayed again and again that with His strength I could continue to sail my seas in a broken vessel not fit for calm water, let alone a cyclone.

Near the end of the second day, the neurosurgeon came into my room and let me know that the fracture in my skull had healed and was no longer leaking.

My relief and my gratitude were beyond any words that I could express.

God's mercy would not end there either. His love would continue through the kindness of so many others who were there to greet me once I got home. Neighbors, family, and friends once again went out of their way to show their love and concern for me. The twelve days of Christmas, paraphernalia from the BYU football team, gifts, meals, service, and visitors all kept me floating during the days of recovery ahead.

Despite the peace and love I felt from my loved ones and especially my Father in Heaven, I was still having acute stress syndrome. Vividly reliving the events of the car crash every time I closed my eyes, much like I'd done after my ATV accident, was horrible. I could hear my tires screeching and see the car coming right at me. The force of the violent accident with its smells and the sounds of bending and twisting steel coursed through my body. To top it off, I had the depressing realization that my life had just been altered yet again. If I couldn't work, what would I do? If I couldn't drive, where would I go?

For many nights after my accident, one of my parents sat in a reclining chair next to my bed all night. Although things had healed and I was incredibly grateful that I would not have to go through brain surgery, the scare was not over yet.

"Brandon, Brandon, wake up! Wake up!" From the sound of my mom's voice, I knew something was very wrong.

It was odd. I could hear and sense the seriousness of her tone, but when I tried to open my eyes and wake up, I couldn't.

"Brandon, we need you to wake up! Start breathing now!" I heard my dad's frantic voice say. "We've called the paramedics! They're on their way!"

It was like I was in a deep coma and could not let my parents know that I could hear them. I fought desperately to move my arm to let them know that I could understand.

"He moved his arm!" I heard my mom yell. "Why aren't his eyes opening, and why isn't he breathing?!"

Someone was lightly slapping my face. "You need to start breathing now!" my parents commanded.

I knew this was serious, but no matter how hard I tried to open my eyes, I could not. I was so exhausted and sleepy.

"It's the medications!" my mom cried. "You're drugged! You need to fight back!"

It took everything for me to force out the barely audible words, "I can hear you."

"Then why aren't you opening your eyes?!" my mom asked sternly.

"I can't breathe!" I replied desperately.

My body felt heavily deprived of oxygen. I fought as hard as I could to open my mouth and start breathing. I was gasping for air and continued to do so for the next five minutes. It felt like I was drowning under water and someone had handed me a tiny coffee straw to breathe through. It was too hard.

I could hear other voices now, but they were distant and muffled.

"He's unresponsive, and his oxygen saturation is very low."

"What's happening?" my mom cried.

"He's having an opiate overdose. We're giving him a shot of naloxone to reverse the effects."

Suddenly air shot through my lungs. Almost immediately and involuntarily, I opened my eyes, totally disoriented.

"Brandon, can you hear us?" a paramedic asked me.

"Yes," I replied.

"Can you tell me where we are?"

"I don't know . . . where I am," I answered, feeling totally confused by the situation.

"Why are we here?"

"I have no idea," I responded.

"How old are you, Brandon?"

"I don't remember," I said, too out of it to feel worried.

By this time, my mom was crying, convinced that the lack of oxygen had had terrible effects on my brain.

I heard one of the paramedics tell my parents that they needed to rush me to the hospital.

Once admitted to the hospital, I remained there for two days. I was told that the dosage and the medicine doctors had prescribed was too powerful for me and had caused me to accidentally overdose. I knew what had happened was life threatening and it was important that I stay in the hospital to be monitored. Still, I just wanted to go home.

When I finally returned home a couple of days later, I was so grateful to be back. People continued to serve me while I spent most of December in bed. In my journal is written a well-known quote attributed to Nelson Mandela that reads, "It's not important how many times you fall but how many times you rise."

After each of my accidents, I have had to "get back up" if I wanted to continue living. Though this was arguably the most minor of my four incidents, it was the one that potentially had the power to completely derail me. With all the time I had spent going to school, all the progress I had made through each of my disabilities, and all the battles I had fought and won, I simply could not move backward. The night of my car accident, when I lay in the hospital bed and heard the song sung by Sting, despite my solid relationship with my Father in Heaven, I waffled.

This was simply too much for me. For years I had acted my part well. I had fought hard. I had tried to be humble, have a good attitude, and help others. Because of that, I guess I thought that I had reached the pinnacle of what would be required of me in this life. It was a low blow when I realized that at any time there could be more for me to go through, more for me to learn, more for me to experience, more pain to feel, more grief, more sorrow. That knowledge was more difficult than many things I had already endured, and the weight of it hung all around me.

As I continued to heal, Christmas drew near, and my anguish grew. I had now gone through my facial reconstruction surgeries and was trying to continue to heal, but I was growing tired of all of it. One night, I lay in bed, once again trying to sleep despite the added pain from the car accident on top of the day-to-day pain I already endured. As all of the horrific memories of my car accident, the ATV, Lake Powell, and my bike accident settled in my mind, pain and fear began to overtake me.

I cried out to my Heavenly Father to please bring me peace, if only momentarily.

In the back of my bruised and broken mind, the last verse to Sting's song that I had sung in the hospital and during many other times when crying out to my Father while pleading for Him to answer my "whys" came to my mind.

"And what would it mean to say that I loved you in my fashion?"[19]

As I let those words sink into my mind, a scripture from Isaiah followed: "For my thoughts are not your thoughts, neither are your ways my ways, saith the Lord. For as the heavens are higher than the earth, so are my ways higher than your ways, and my thoughts than your thoughts" (Isaiah 55:8–9).

As tears streamed down my face, I once again understood that everything I had gone through had brought me so much closer to God than I ever could have been without it. I could

---

19. "Why Should I Cry for You?"

not deny that. God had allowed my tiny ship to be sent out to sea and tossed in the waves, knowing it was never sea-worthy.

With His infinite grace and understanding, only He understood the price I would need to pay to know Him so much better than I could otherwise and to feel His love more deeply than I ever thought possible. To know the whisperings of His spirit so well that I would never doubt them. To stand as His witness. To feel of His majesty. For all these things to be possible, my vessel would have to break, over and over and over again, but that was what He always intended.

For God loves broken things . . . and broken things love God.

Chapter 21

WE ARE ALL PARALYZED

Although somewhere in the back of my head I knew it was not possible, my plan was to return to work. There was no other choice in my mind. My boss graciously offered to hold my job position open for sixty days. Before I left work for the last time, I went upstairs and visited with each of the employees, promising that I would return well before my allotted sixty days were up.

My first priority was ordering a new truck. It arrived within a month. The only difference was the color. This time, it was white. Excited, I raced down with my dad to the shop to pick it up. As soon as I had the keys, my dad walked over to watch me get inside.

As I started my transfer, it was immediately evident that I could not lift myself. Panic began to edge its way inside of me. My left side, particularly my left arm, was weaker from the accident. I hadn't understood the extent until I was able to try transferring for the first time since the accident.

Seeing my deflated expression, my dad immediately chimed in. "You learned how to transfer once, and you can do it again," he said confidently. "It'll come back to you, and so will the feeling in your left side."

Although I longed to believe him, in my heart I felt an alarm go off. The facial surgeons that had just done my reconstructive surgery had warned me that using my head to transfer was incredibly dangerous. One false placement could not only undo all that the surgery had just fixed but could also cause my brain to leak spinal fluid again. This would result in the brain surgery I had just begged God to save me from. There was a strong possibility I would never drive again. I put the thought far from my mind as my dad helped me into the truck and I drove home.

The next day I started practicing transferring again. Whereas before I had the strength but didn't know how to transfer, this time I knew how to transfer but lacked the strength. Few things were harder for me to accept than that the freedom I had worked so hard to obtain was once again gone.

When my sixty days were almost up, I reluctantly spoke to my employers, who were gracious in their offer to extend the job opening for me. As I brainstormed other ideas of how to get to work, I finally began to acknowledge that there really was no way that I would be able to return. I knew well from my relationship with my Heavenly Father that He had a plan for me and that this, although difficult, played a part. Turning the situation over to Him, I asked God to point me to a new door and the next path He wanted me to take. Then with a heavy heart, I let my employers know that I would not be coming back.

Not only was that difficult, but my face and arm were still numb from the accident. With little good real estate still available on my body, I hoped that the one place that I could feel touch would not remain numb. If God decided to take that from me, I knew I would really struggle. Feeling did eventually return to most of my face, but it was a difficult and scary time waiting. Feeling a little like Job from the Bible, I wondered if God would take everything from me as well.

My good days are what most people would consider a living nightmare. After I broke my neck, everything changed—and I mean *everything*. Most people probably don't understand the extent to which my independence was taken from me after I became paralyzed. To be frank, it's quite depressing and embarrassing to talk about. One might see me in my wheelchair and see my limitations as just that of pushing instead of walking. Unfortunately, that's just the tip of my iceberg. My morning routine is a prime example.

I lie motionless in bed. My eyes are open and looking nervously at the clock on my bedroom dresser as I wait. I want to get out of bed to start my day, but I have to wait on someone else. Sometimes the aides come at 7:30 a.m.; sometimes it's not until 9:00. It all depends on their schedules. I think about how my life was and how my life should be. The inevitable tears begin to fill my eyes. They cascade down my cheeks in a pattern so familiar that it almost happens involuntarily now.

My mind races, and I wonder who will be coming this time. I get nervous thinking that maybe it's somebody new— or worse, maybe it's a woman, which is always embarrassing for me. What if it's a new person altogether, who doesn't know what they are doing?

My bladder is full, and my heart has begun to pound from needing to go to the bathroom. I try to remember how I used to do all of this with ease, but it has long become a distant memory.

My home health aide finally arrives. I breathe a sigh of relief. This time it's an aide who has been here before. I have him quickly grab a catheter in my bathroom drawer and the urinal. Once he has it, he inserts the catheter, relieving the pressure of my very full bladder. I smile and thank him, but inside it's a personal hell trying to make sense of it all. I also know that this horrid process is just getting started.

As if he can sense my thoughts, he begins to remove my clothing before rolling me on my back. My bladder isn't the only thing that needs to be relieved. Today is Monday, which means it's my bowel care day. My aide goes back to my bathroom and grabs a handful of suppositories. I take a deep breath, unnoticeable to him, and prepare myself for this necessary but humiliating task. He puts on his plastic gloves, while silent tears again make their way down my cheeks. I'm grateful he cannot see my face. Neither of us speaks now.

After a little while, he asks me what I would like to wear. I point with confidence to the couch in my room, where the outfit I have chosen the night before is laid out. That's one thing that I get to choose and control in this morning of utter reliance, and I live for it.

Forty-five minutes pass before he helps transfer me to my shower chair at the side of my bed. I'm completely naked both inside and out as my aide pushes me into the shower. He hands me a washcloth so I can wash the areas that I am able to, before he finishes the job. I dry off with towels before heading back to my bedroom, where I'm again transferred into bed.

This time my aide helps me get dressed. Afterward, he moves my legs around, stretching and pulling them. If I'm not stretched out regularly, my legs get very tight, making transfers to and from my wheelchair harder to manage.

Once I am in my wheelchair, my aide helps me put on and tuck in my shirt. Finally, I'm able to do something I can do independently: brush my teeth and comb my hair. Meanwhile, my aide goes to the kitchen to help make me breakfast.

After all of this, two to three hours have passed, and we are finally done. I always thank my aide for his love and care in helping me get ready that morning, knowing that I'll be seeing him again too soon and we'll start this process all over tomorrow morning.

Finally up and alone, I feed my dog, Buddy, who has been my constant companion and lifeline. Now I am ready to start my day.

Throughout the day I have to cath myself, something I am grateful I am able to do on my own. I do it every four to five hours to relieve my bladder. This process can take anywhere from five to twenty minutes.

Since breaking my neck, everything in my life is horribly challenging. As time goes by, my desire for the independence I had when I was eighteen does not fade; it only grows stronger. It's been almost twenty years of this routine, and I still haven't gotten used to it. Every morning is a cruel reminder of how physically disabled I truly am. Sometimes things are better left unsaid, but this is my reality.

Once night hits, my parents help me transfer into bed. They remove my pants and cover me with blankets. Buddy, who has been with me as long as I have endured this routine, snuggles up to me, unaware and unconcerned that I am paralyzed. As I pull Buddy close to me, I hope that tonight my dreams will take me places where my disability doesn't follow. The nights when I am reminded what being physically independent once felt like are my favorite nights.

For now, I will need to wait for independence to return to me. Like that Eagles song, "I've been waiting in the weeds, waiting for my time to come back around again."[20]

Despite all of that and the many other challenges I have had to face in my life, I do not want to be known as someone who gave up or wallowed in my trial. There are no redos in this life, and this is the life I have been given. I still get to choose how I respond to it. There is a quote that I love from the movie *Gladiator* that says, "What we do in life echoes in eternity."[21] I don't want anything I've said or done negatively reverberating in this life. I don't want it ever said about me that I gave up instead of fighting, or even that I backed down.

That first night in the hospital after my spinal injury, I sang "Come Thou Fount of Every Blessing" while vowing to raise my Ebenezer. I hope I have done that in the twenty years that have passed since. The Lord helped me that night, and He has continued to help me through the years each time I have needed Him. I don't know why I've had to go through so many painful experiences and live through their long-term effects. I've lost many tears and sleepless nights wondering. I have been humbled and broken mentally, physically, psychologically, and spiritually.

Mother Teresa once said, "We must know exactly when we say yes to God what is in that yes. Yes means 'I surrender,' totally, fully, without any counting the cost, without any examination: 'Is it all right? Is it convenient?' Our yes to God is without any reservations."[22]

---

20. "Waiting in the Weeds," track 7 on *Long Road Out of Eden*, Lost Highway Records, 2007.
21. *Gladiator*, directed by Ridley Scott (2000; DreamWorks Pictures).
22. *Jesus, the Word to Be Spoken*, compiled by Father Angelo D. Scolozzi.

In the end, no matter how hard my life has been, I cannot deny that all of this has made me a better person and brought me closer to God. As long as I choose to see my life and my experiences and my challenges through the eyes of a loving Heavenly Father and Savior Jesus Christ, while trying to help others see that as well, my life has meaning and purpose.

While I was working at IMC, I gave every patient that I met a handout. On it was written a well-known story that I'd once read about King Louis XVI of France.

> Many years ago I heard the story of the son of King Louis XVI of France. King Louis had been taken from his throne and imprisoned. His young son, the prince, was taken by those who dethroned the king. They thought that inasmuch as the king's son was heir to the throne, if they could destroy him morally, he would never realize the great and grand destiny that life had bestowed upon him.
>
> They took him to a community far away, and there they exposed the lad to every filthy and vile thing that life could offer. They exposed him to foods the richness of which would quickly make him a slave to appetite. They used vile language around him constantly. They exposed him to lewd and lusting women. They exposed him to dishonor and distrust. He was surrounded 24 hours a day by everything that could drag the soul of a man as low as one could slip. For over six months he had this treatment—but not once did the young lad buckle under pressure. Finally, after intensive temptation, they questioned him. Why had he not submitted himself to these things—why had he not partaken? These things would provide pleasure, satisfy his lusts, and were desirable; they were all his. The boy said, "I cannot do what you ask for I was born to be a king."

We are all born to be kings in the kingdom of God.[23]

After giving the handout to my patients and telling them the story, I'd always ask the same question: "Who will you decide to be today?"

I had patients who at times would say, "Brandon, I don't believe in God. This story is pointless."

I would quickly reply, "My friend, there is no such thing as an atheist in a foxhole. You are in the battle of your life. Now would be a good time to find out how much God loves you."

It is only when we gain proper vision of who we truly are and where we are going after this life that we can see beyond our mortal trials. We are not merely born to be what our circumstances give us. We are born to be queens and kings.

I'll never forget a time when I was asked to speak at a juvenile detention center and the Lord taught me this beautiful principle firsthand.

When I arrived at the center, I grimaced as I looked at the building; it looked like it had been built to house captives. Like a Roman barrack, it was constructed like a rock, with no outside windows where light could reach its occupants.

On my way inside the building, I had to pass through four steel doors and then another made of thick bulletproof glass. The whole compound was heavily fortified and guarded to protect the youth it housed, from themselves as well as from others, and to protect those of us from the outside world who might enter into its unforgiving and gloomy walls.

---

23. Vaughn J. Featherstone, "The King's Son," *New Era*, Nov. 1975.

A couple of the guards greeted me before taking me to one of their vacant cells. I was immediately overcome with emotion. There in front of me stood a three-by-five-foot cement room. There were no windows. No comfort from home displayed on the walls. They had access to nothing but a toilet and a cold cot.

What kind of child could possibly be sentenced to live here? I wondered.

As if in response, the guards began to warn me about the group of juveniles and their bad behaviors. They told me I should not be caught off guard when the kids decided to scream at me or flip me off during my presentation and assured me that would happen regardless of my message or what I looked like. They would not care.

I was a bit nervous, and honestly a little excited, to see what type of reaction I would get.

As I sat alone on the stand, I waited for their arrival. Not too long after, I watched kids ranging from twelve to eighteen years old file into the room. Chained and cuffed, they were separated by offense and by gender. All together they totaled 250 children of various ethnicities, from various social classes and backgrounds. As my eyes studied them, I noted how very young they all were.

An interesting dynamic was at play as I watched them walk in. I knew they were yearning for their physical independence and autonomy. I recognized their looks of desperation as they longed to be free from their prison. The parallels between us hit me: they yearned for my freedom—the ability that I had to leave this place—while I watched their legs and longed to be able to move on my own. I saw how we all longed to be free from the various ailments that plagued us. I sobered as I realized that their prison could be mine too, if I allowed it to be, just as mine could be theirs.

It was time for me to speak. I felt somewhat unsteady and unsure of my message. Looking down at my notes, I set them aside. Instead, I began by sharing with them how I became paralyzed. I told them how I try not to let my paralyzing circumstance paralyze me mentally, socially, and spiritually. I taught them how they too could overcome their individual trials and weaknesses.

I then testified to them of the overwhelming love Jesus Christ has for each and every one of them. It wasn't just words coming out of my mouth either. I felt the truthfulness of that message radiate inside me. It was as if I had just been given a small taste of the compassion and love Christ has for them—for every single one of us. As I felt that love fill my entire being, I made them a promise: if they came unto Him in faith and deed, He would help them individually by giving them the strength and wisdom needed to defeat their past and pave a bright future ahead, just as He was doing for me.

While I spoke, I hadn't focused on any one person, choosing instead to look out at the large audience as one big group. Now, as I finished, I looked around at each of them, fearful of what the repercussions of my message would be. I braced myself for the swear words and threats that the guards had assured me would come.

They never did.

Instead, I watched in amazement as many of the guards and service volunteers that had helped put on this speaking event stood there stunned by the reaction they saw from the juveniles. Many of the kids had tears streaming down their faces as if they were hearing truth for the first time in their short lives.

They had intensely listened to me, hanging on my every word. Not only that, but they were smiling at me. I could see hope in their faces and newfound encouragement. I sat humbled at the honor I'd just had to be able to pass on a message from a Heavenly Father who loved them in a way that this group of "unlovable" children could not understand. In a matter of moments, their hard exteriors had softened, now reflecting happiness and hope as they saw a path where they could overcome their obstacles and challenges, instead of their obstacles overcoming them.

I noticed one of the juveniles ask something to the guard near him. The guard hesitated for a moment. Soon others were nodding around him. The guard came forward and asked me if it would be all right for the youth to be uncuffed long enough to shake my hand.

Emotion caught in my throat. I could only nod, completely blown away at what was happening. Two hundred fifty of God's children then lined up to shake my hand or hug me. They expressed humble words of thanks for telling them that they had not been forgotten, in spite of choices they had made.

To this day, my most captive audience has been a young group of kids in captivity.

As they funneled out of the room, fresh tears raced down my cheeks as I sat in humble reverence at the lesson I had just been privileged to be a part of. These kids were no different than me. Both of us had a Heavenly Father who loved us, despite our choices, weaknesses, and even our love for Him in return.

As I watched them go, the Spirit whispered to me, *Some of us are paralyzed by accidents and some by our own doing. But just the same, we are all paralyzed.*

Chapter 22

THE JOURNEY

The idea for participating in a race started after I graduated from college. I missed exercising and the endorphins that filled my body mixed with the sense of accomplishment it brings. I approached my parents with the idea, and they were immediately on board. The one concern they had was keeping me cool since the race would be on July 24. As it got later in the day, we all knew the temperatures could reach over 100 degrees.

"Remember, Brandon, you have no internal air conditioner," my mom was saying. "I don't want you going alone. You'll overheat and pass out."

She was right too. After my spinal cord injury, I couldn't sweat, no matter how hard I worked out or how hot it was outside. This has been a life-threatening challenge for me. There have been a few times I've nearly died from heatstroke.

Regardless of the concerns, I had to sign up. I knew I could finish the race, but I also understood that I would need somebody with me who could protect me from the heat that I couldn't handle on my own. The person I wanted by my side was Bronson. Even as I thought it, I heard Bronson promise our mom, "I'm going. I won't leave his side. I'll make sure he's okay."

With my mom feeling better about the idea, the next step was to purchase a hand cycle. The bike I would use would sit low to the ground. Velcro would keep my hands strapped to the hand pedals. The only difference between this bike and traditional bikes was that my hands instead of my feet would be used to propel it forward. Once I had my bike, I signed up for the 10K race as part of Salt Lake City's annual Pioneer Day celebration, and training officially began.

I trained tirelessly, working out and learning about the course and its obstacles so that I could gain better insight into what difficulties I would no doubt encounter along the way.

The morning of the race arrived, bringing with it the heat of summer. Known in Utah as Pioneer Day, it was one of my favorite holidays. I had grown up loving this holiday, as did many people in Utah. Most Utah-owned businesses close on July 24 as family and friends gather together to barbecue, watch fireworks, and go to the extraordinary Days of '47 parade in downtown Salt Lake City. The parade route also happened to be where my race would end. One could argue this holiday may even be bigger for many Utahans than the Fourth of July. I knew the race and the events would be well attended.

On July 24, 1847, the first group of pioneers finally arrived in the Salt Lake Valley after escaping religious persecution. Their incredible journey on foot from Nauvoo, Illinois, to Salt Lake City, Utah, was arduous and plagued by sorrow and death.

I already had a special reverence for those who had gone before me, enabling me to live in this beautiful Salt Lake Valley that I called home. To be a part of the race experience while celebrating a day in honor of those pioneers was awesome.

On the day of the race, I could feel the familiar adrenaline pump through my heart, mingled with a desire to have those old feelings of competition pour through my body. As we got to the starting line, I knew where I wanted to be. Innately competitive, I had to be in the front, not only leading the pack but also leaving them all far behind me. What had caught my attention in picking this course was its start. It was entirely downhill for the first mile and a half.

I was so incredibly sick of being passed in life. At how many races, basketball games, and sporting events had I been the one out front, the one to watch, before my neck injury? I was ready to go back to the old Brandon, the one that showed everyone else how it was done, even if just for a day. "I'm going to smoke them all," I had told my parents with a smile.

Now we were finally here, and I was out in front where I belonged. I smiled at Bronson, who sat on his mountain bike, laden with both water and spray bottles as if he were my Sherpa and I were about to climb Everest. Bronson smiled back at me and gave me some words of encouragement while assuring me he would be right by my side. A memory pushed through the back of my mind as I watched Bronson on his bike, ready at any moment to answer my call of need.

"Brandon, help me! Help me!" I could hear my little brother screaming in panic as a bully began to pursue him. I had been playing soccer during recess when I heard Bronson, who was then a first grader, cry out. Only a year and a half apart in age, we were inseparable and each other's best friends. While I was always bigger and stronger when we were growing up, he was usually the smallest in his grade, often incurring the wrath of the bigger kids in his classes.

Hearing his cry for help, I immediately stopped what I was doing. I began to run as fast as I could toward the sounds while shouting, "Bronson, run toward me!"

One thing Bronson was good at in his youth was running fast. Like an antelope, he'd run quickly, dodging right and left, swiftly trying to outrun his pursuers, while leading the lions right to me. This time the bully met my fist as I fought off the attack. This happened on various occasions through elementary and junior high school. Eventually kids at school realized if they picked on Bronson, they'd have to contend with his big brother.

Love poured through me for my little brother, who was now both bigger and stronger than me. This time it was I who had a significant weakness compared to the strength of those who surrounded me. I was grateful he would be there by my side as he had been my entire life.

My mind came back to the moment as I watched men and women fill in the gaps behind me. My eyes watched their legs. It's funny how I had long ago stopped studying faces. I was now obsessed with legs. Tall and athletic, their muscles bulged with ridges that outlined and defined each separate grouping. These were the athletes, those that were most definitely not running their first race. As they shook out their quads in preparation for takeoff, I watched their muscles move obediently back and forth in response. As I considered their movements, I knew me doing a 10K wasn't just about proving to myself that I was just as good as I once was—it was also about letting the world know as well, since they had long since forgotten. Visions of me pushing across the finish line and coming in first swirled in my mind, coursing new adrenaline through my soul.

The sound of a gunshot pierced the still morning air.

"Later, guys! Try to keep up!" I yelled to no one in particular but to everyone willing to hear. With a winning smile, I took off like a rocket. Flanked by some of the best long-distance runners in the nation, I heaved my arms forward as their legs propelled them in the same direction.

The starting line was high on the Salt Lake Valley bench with the vertical Wasatch Mountains behind us. Because of the downhill slope that started us out, I knew I had the advantage. Below us the Salt Lake Valley was in full bloom. The finish line was just over six miles down the road, and we all wanted to reach it. I just wanted to get there first.

When you can't run or even walk, you dream about both often. After more than a decade of running in my dreams, I was ready to run awake. Before my spinal cord injury, I'd excelled at running long distances, so I reasoned, why not try it again? However, all the practice of running in my dreams without tiring gave me a false sense of confidence. This led me shooting out of the gate a lot faster than I'd ever gone before. As I blazed past everyone, I figured I would just roll through this race and let my arms do the running.

Experiencing the high of pushing your body to its limits wakes you, making you feel alive and free, as if your spirit and body are one in purpose. Having a spirit that's fully independent but trapped inside a physical body unwilling to match its desired freedom is maddening. Here was my chance to wake my body from its long slumber.

The other runners quickly fell behind. Even Bronson, on his bike, was having a difficult time keeping up with me as I reached speeds close to twenty-five miles per hour. I knew this was the only place that I could get the advantage amongst the other runners, and I made the most of it. With just over a mile of my race down, I saw that the road began to flatten. This would be where my journey would truly begin. At least five minutes ahead of everyone else, I began to move slower every block I traveled. The summer sun quickly turned from warm to hot to scorching as the 15 percent of usable muscle in my arms protested its insurmountable task. The further I went, the harder the sun beat down on me. Immediately, I realized that though I had put in ample preparation for this day, it would not matter. I had not understood how hard this race would be for my body to accomplish.

Reluctantly, I had to stop.

Bronson, please hurry and help me. I'm burning up, I urgently thought.

From the time we were kids, Bronson had never left my side. After my head injury as a child, my reasoning became sporadic and impulsive, causing me at times not to think before I reacted. Add that to a teenage mind, and I needed a voice of reason. Bronson was that voice. When I was getting into mischief, which was often, he'd warn me not to do whatever I was thinking of doing. I'd do it anyway. He'd come along and try his hardest to talk some sense into me, knowing he would never change my mind and that whatever trouble I got into, he would pay for it as well. I never did heed his warnings, just as he never stopped coming with me. Bronson once joked that he'd spent his entire childhood running from things he didn't do, followed by a roll of his eyes and an exasperated comment, "I was even attacked by a dog . . . twice!"

I protected Bronson physically (well except for from the dogs) while he protected me mentally. He still does that for me. He is always the one who leads me out of the darkness. He reminds me of how strong I can be while showing me the eternal perspective. "You are going to be so much further ahead for what you've gone through," he'll tell me, never once judging me. He's there as many times as I need him to be. After Bronson got married, he made a promise to me: "I will never live further than a block away, and my children will be your children."

Bronson lives half a mile down the road from my house, where his children are often seen playing with their uncle.

There are myriad times Bronson has been there to save me, whether a feeling told him he needed to get home, only for him to find I had fallen out of my wheelchair or was going into dysreflexia, or life had simply gotten too hard and I couldn't be alone.

Moses had Aaron, David had Jonathan, and I have Bronson.

Even as I thought about how he'd never left my side, my brother was suddenly there. Jumping from his bike, he sprang into action, grabbing ice-cold water bottles for me to drink and spraying me down.

As the artificial sweat ran down my neck, I breathed a sigh of relief.

Behind me, I could hear the pack of legs running not only to catch up with me, their leader, but also to overtake me. These guys were coming fast. They seemed to have no weaknesses holding them back either. Panic consumed me. *I cannot get passed*. I knew it was silly even as I thought it, but I needed to come in first, and as absurd as it was for me to think that, I had genuinely thought my will would be enough to get me there.

"I'm right behind you," I heard Bronson say. "You can do this!" His confidence in me and his support gave me the assurance I needed to keep cranking my hand pedals forward. In the back of my mind, though, I now knew that I wouldn't come in first and that I had a long way to go yet.

A whisper inside my soul spoke peace to my mind. *Don't worry. It doesn't matter how fast you can run. What matters is successfully crossing the finish line. It's not when you finish; it's how you finish that matters. Just get there. Your family and loved ones will be there waiting.*

Tears filled my eyes as first one and then another and then many legs ran past me. No longer an option that I beat everyone else, I now understood that no one but me ever cared what place I took. They had all just come to watch me finish the race. I knew my parents and family were anxiously waiting for me on the other side of the finish line. I had to finish strong. I was determined to make it, no matter how hard the difficulties of the journey were. Besides, I had been through far harder things and had come out on top. This would be no different. As I continued to push, I made a new goal free of any stipulations: I would simply finish the race.

Still, I wanted to blend in with the crowd. If I was left too far behind, then I became "that poor, pitiful kid," and I was sick of being looked at like that. I had signed up for this race to give myself a win, and now I was afraid it was going to be the opposite—one more thing that showed my weaknesses to everybody. It wasn't about the runners passing me either. It was the people like me, those who were paraplegics also pushing with their hands, that got in my head. I knew it was ridiculous to compare myself to them. Their arms were not paralyzed like mine, and they had full muscle function above their waists. Still, when I looked at them, I saw me and couldn't help but compare myself. As I inched forward, I fluctuated between negative feelings of comparison and the overwhelming sensation that I still had so far to go.

Miles stretched longer and longer as the day dragged on and the sun grew hotter. I looked at Bronson, his face reflecting encouragement while my face was filled with pain and frustration. My forearms screamed that I could not possibly go on. I became lost in the thoughts that swirled inside my mind. Despite aching muscles, I continued, while wondering if unseen angels were beside me. In response, another refreshing blast from the spray bottle hit my neck. Taking a water bottle from his backpack, Bronson held it to my lips. Surely Bronson is one of my angels who have been assigned to watch over me here on this Earth, even as I once watched over him.

Despite the feelings of the Spirit that accompanied me off and on during that race, I was going so slow that at times I wondered if I would ever make it. My strength was leaving me, and I wanted to stop. Once again, my Spirit willed me inwardly as it showed me the countless other times I had wanted to give up.

"Brandon, stay with me!" a nurse commanded. "Don't you leave us!"

My thirteen-year-old head had been pounding as I fought to stay present, while the appeal of unconsciousness beckoned me to follow, giving me some relief from the excruciating pain. I was being raced from the emergency room twenty-four hours after my bicycle accident to the waiting Life Flight helicopter. One of the nurses on board spoke to me again while we were taking off.

"Brandon, stay with me!"

My mind continued to tug at me to revisit the memories, so as not to focus on the pain burning inside my biceps as I continued to push forward, despite everything screaming at me to end this impossible journey.

Suddenly I was back in Lake Powell surrounded by water on all sides, lying face up.

"Brandon, stay with me," my mom cried. "Don't you leave us! We love you!"

One of the nurses flying me out of Lake Powell, once again in a Life Flight helicopter, would also plead with me.

"Don't close your eyes and drift off, Brandon," she said. "Stay with me."

When I had collided head-on with another car on the freeway and as I was being taken from my truck on a stretcher, one of the paramedics would shout to me.

"Brandon, stay with me."

Later when I would return home from the car accident, I would fight to come back after an accidental overdose only to hear my mom screaming.

"Brandon! Stay with me!"

Those words would again come to me when I wanted to end it all after rolling my ATV and again while fishing for king salmon in Alaska after losing my grip on life.

I felt the power of those memories move through me as Bronson now walked by my side, my pace now too slow for him to use his bike.

Once again, I gazed at my brother. In my mind, I saw a little first grader screaming and running toward me on the playground. "Brandon, help me!" he had called out to me.

"Bronson, run toward me!" I had called out in response.

Tears filled my eyes as I heard the voice again. This time I imagined it spoken to me by another loving brother.

"Run toward me, Brandon," I imagined my Savior and elder brother, Jesus Christ, lovingly whisper to me. "Stay with me."

As I pushed pedals hot with the sun's rays, I looked down the road and said out loud: "Brandon, stay with me. We still have work yet to do."

Finding a little strength, I continued to crank my hand pedals as the steady stream of people passing me by became smaller and smaller.

Only a mile away from the finish line, we turned onto 200 East in Salt Lake City. With my head down, I began to breathe deeply, focusing on pushing myself slowly over every white line, spaced ten feet apart, in the center of the road. I crawled forward, each push of my wheel feeling like my last. As the miles grew in length, the minutes ticked away, making each one feel longer than the one before. I was absolutely done physically, but I refused to give up. Willing my body to do the impossible, I kept going, despite having already given everything, all while praying for angels to assist me.

And suddenly they were there.

A roar of voices called to me from the sidelines as people began cheering for me with one voice. "Keep going! You can do it!"

Astonished, I raised my head from its bent-over position to see where the sound was coming from.

People I did not know, who had come to watch the parade, thousands of them on both sides of the road, were standing up in unison and cheering for me.

"Keep going!" they screamed as if they could push me forward with their words. "You can do it!"

Emotion consumed me. I kept nodding my head in appreciation for these earthly angels and their support and love. Humbled, I turned the last corner of my race. There in front of me, excitedly jumping up and down and waving to me, were my parents, just on the other side of my finish line.

With tears of happiness, I rolled over the finish line before slumping in a heap of exhaustion. I had finished my race on July 24. The same date I had become paralyzed.

Together my family and I celebrated. I had finally made it.

Perhaps equally important was not just that I had made it but that someone was waiting for me at the end. It wasn't until a little while later that I wondered where Bronson was. I would then learn that when the spectators started to cheer me on, Bronson had quietly slipped away, saying later that it didn't make sense for him to be there anymore. He had played his part.

All of us will cross our own finish line and return to the loving arms of our family, our friends, and our Heavenly Father, who are there waiting for us. All of us will have angels both in heaven and on earth, who will slip in and out of our lives when we need them the most.

When I started my race, my goal was simple: I wanted to beat everyone else. When I finished, I realized my race was a journey, and it had never been about a single day.

All of us have been running the race of life since we were born. Some of us are yet to cross our finish lines, but we all will one day. It is inherent in us, this longing to return home. It really doesn't matter how fast we go either; it's the direction we are moving. God simply expects us to finish.

God doesn't compare me to the other runners either. He knows that He has blessed them with legs and our race is not a fair one, nor was it ever designed to be. I too have been blessed in other ways they have not. He didn't put us all in the same race so that He could keep score and watch us compete. And if that is the case, then surely it wasn't His design to have us compare our progress with each other's.

God put us in the race together because He knew we would need someone to make sure we finished. He knew we would need a brother by our side, someone to say, "Stay with me," when our race becomes unbearable.

As often as I heard this command while I was suffering and dying, I have said it even more to myself when I have been depressed and heartbroken. When my mind wanders down dark paths, I immediately say, "Brandon, stay with me!" I know that if I focus on who I truly am, I'll have the strength needed to successfully finish this journey and cross the finish line amongst my friends and family before running into the arms of my loving Savior and Brother. Then my Master will say: "Well done, thou good and faithful servant: thou hast been faithful over a few things, I will make thee ruler over many things: enter thou into the joy of thy Lord" (Matthew 25:21).

Epilogue

Upon completion of this book, I submitted the manuscript to various publishers. One day I heard back from a publisher who informed me that they had decided to pass on my book. When I asked for feedback as to why, she apologetically explained that their editors ultimately felt that the book didn't leave them feeling uplifted or inspired.

Thankfully that was not the response I had received from others, so I didn't worry about it too much. However, it did get me thinking. What *were* those readers looking for? Immediately when I had that thought, I knew the answer. They wanted everything I'd had to endure, everything I had not been given, and everything that I had lost to make sense. In short, they wanted a happy ending.

There was a missing chapter. Where was my wife? Where were my kids? Where were my riches? My independence and my redemption? If the book did not end with, "Then I found the girl of my dreams, we got married, had a family, and I walked miraculously away from my wheelchair," then how could my story possibly be inspiring? After all, living with pain daily is anything but.

To be fair to those editors, that is a question I still ask myself daily. Likely I am not the only one. Any of us who have constant struggles are all too familiar with tragedies that are far too lengthy and restitution that seems a lifetime away. Perhaps the better question is not about *where* my kids, wife, independence, and happy ending are, but *when*.

One of my favorite movies is *Gladiator*. There is an insightful scene in the movie that I feel sums up my life seamlessly. In this scene, the main character, Maximus, and his friend Juba are talking about their families. Maximus's wife and son were killed years previously. Juba was captured and made a slave and likely will not see his family again. The two men discuss their profound losses and their longing to be reunited with their loved ones.

While looking out over the landscape, Juba remarks to Maximus that somewhere out there is his country and his family. "Will I ever see them again?" he says. "I think no."

Maximus then responds, "Do you believe you'll see them again when you die?"

Juba nods and says, "I think so, but then I will die soon. They will not die for many years. I'll have to wait."

"But you would? Wait?" Maximus asks.

"Of course," Juba responds.

Maximus then explains, "You see, my wife and my son are already waiting for me."

Juba smiles at his friend. Speaking with assurance, he says, "You will meet them again, but not yet." He pauses before briefly repeating, "Not yet," as if to say to Maximus that there is work yet for him to do in this life.

Maximus nods his head as if he already knows. He then whispers, "Not yet. Not yet," reconfirming to himself that he must wait, though he longs for nothing more than to be reunited with his wife and child.[24]

Besides those profound words, one of the things I love about this scene is the look on Juba's face when he speaks them. Despite all they both have endured and lost, the look is one of peace, filled with hope for what is to come but is not yet.

All of us experience *not yet* in various forms. We hope for better jobs, better health, better circumstances. We hope to reclaim what was taken from us or what we lost. We hope for things to make sense one day and for better understanding. In short, we hope for a happy ending.

Countless times I feel as though I am not living life or that it is passing me by, without acknowledging or realizing that the very essence of all I am enduring *is* life. How can we fully appreciate happy endings if we do not at some point experience devastating beginnings, middles, and even ends?

It is not *why* the righteous suffer. It is *how*.

In the book of Job, heartache strikes in the very first chapter when a messenger shows up at Job's door and tells him that his servants have been killed and his livestock stolen. The next three verses all begin the same way: "While he was yet speaking, there came also another . . ." (Job 1:16).

Job doesn't get a chance to breathe or process what has just happened before the next trial hits with full force. His door remains open as messenger after messenger comes running to tell him how his life is being completely decimated in rapid succession.

After we read verse after verse of unfathomable destruction, we read what is perhaps one of the most profound verses written in that book.

---

24. *Gladiator*, directed by Ridley Scott (2000; DreamWorks Pictures).

"Then Job arose, and rent his mantle, and shaved his head, and fell down upon the ground, and worshipped, . . . the Lord gave, and the Lord hath taken away; blessed be the name of the Lord" (Job 1:20, 21).

How can it be that someone can go through so much and then fall to his knees, not to scream, not to cry out, not even to ask why, but to worship the very Being who has allowed this to happen to a "just and perfect man"?

Finally, having lost all, Job curses the circumstances of his birth and his very life. Yet he never once curses his Heavenly Father. Instead, he testifies that his Redeemer lives and that Job himself will be resurrected, and in his flesh, he will see God. He testifies that all will be made right . . . eventually.

Like Job, I have often cursed the circumstances of my birth. Why does it seem that while I am dealing with one major obstacle, yet cometh another to tell me of something else I must endure?

In the past two years, while I was writing this book, life's uninvited messengers continued to show up at my door regularly. They came in the form of self-doubt, pain, sickness, depression, having my entire life savings stolen from my investment account, and more. Yet at the same time, I also experienced premonitions, thoughts, and even angels whispering to me the words that make up not only this book but also my very life.

After reading forty-two chapters of how Job has suffered, we finally get to read, "And the Lord turned the captivity of Job, . . . [and] gave Job twice as much as he had before. . . . So the Lord blessed the later end of Job more than his beginning" (Job 42:10, 12).

I think it's important to note that the Lord didn't just bless Job with twice as many riches or blessings as he'd had before. Because of all Job had gone through, his spiritual growth was infinitely more than it would have been having not experienced all the loss. It is the same with me.

I do not doubt that I, like Job, will have everything and more restored to me eventually, just as I cannot deny that the spiritual growth I have experienced because of my trials is of infinite worth. But all of this comes at a price. Job's life could've just been a horrible, sad, and yes, even uninspiring story, but because he chose to trust and love God, Job's circumstances didn't dictate his outcome—he did.

In my mind, I am leaving this book unfinished. There is another chapter that I long to write and know that I will one day. It will be a chapter filled with lasting resolution, love, and peace.

That day I will be free, but I will have to wait.

It is coming . . . but not yet. Not yet.

Acknowledgments

I have to start out by thanking my parents. I would not be who I am without them. My loving dad and mom have patiently borne my adversities on their strong shoulders. I have relied on both of them countless times for loving service and counsel. For my loving brother and best friend, Bronson, who has always had my back and supported me when I was at my lowest moments in life. To my two sisters, Bridgett and Brittney, who I will always be indebted to for their love and service, and to my siblings' spouses, who are more brothers and sister to me than in-laws. Thank you Chris, Cory, and Charlee for your loving patience.

A special and heartfelt thank you to my cherished friend Bruce Porter for encouraging me to write a book. Bruce believed in my story so deeply that he began writing possible chapters for me years ago. He wanted to call that book Where Eagles Fly. Bruce passed on a little while into his project and did not know that a book telling my story would finally come to fruition years later. I know that Bruce has been one of those angels on the other side that have helped compile the spirit of this message. I cannot wait to one day fly with you amongst the eagles.

To Kate Lee, my co-author and dear high school friend. We spent many long hours crying together, being inspired by the Spirit. Without Kate's help, this book would not have gotten off the ground. Thank you for believing in me and in the story and for the many hours spent on the book. I'm so grateful that I had you by my side during the process of telling my story.

A special thanks to my publisher, editors, and many others at Cedar Fort who believed in me and in my story—especially to Kathryn Watkins, who fought for it to be published.

There are far too many people who have been there for me to thank them one by one. You have read my stories, encouraged their telling, taught me in my youth to my adult years, loved me, guided me, served me, cried for and with me, worked alongside me, and much more. If you have ever been affiliated with me in some way or manner, then you have touched my life for the better. Thank you.

Lastly, to my loving Heavenly Father and my Savior, who have always been there for me, who have saved me from death and stood by me in despair. They are my strength, my heavenly grace, and the very reason I can move forward through seemingly impossible and unbearable trials. I know that They know me personally and that one day I will stand before Them whole.

—Brandon

I would like to thank my dear friend Brandon for graciously and bravely allowing me into your life to see, feel, and experience your sorrows, grief, trials, faith, and testimony. It has been my privilege and a priceless gift that has altered my life forever. Thank you to my wonderful husband and four children for supporting me as I've spent time working on this incredible project. Thank you to the many friends and family who read and re-read the numerous drafts and supported us. I am especially grateful to my Father in Heaven, who generously poured out His spirit and allowed us to borrow heaven's words to create this book.

—Kate